SAFE TRAVEL ABROAD

Integrated Protective Concepts

Text copyright © 2012 Integrated Protective Concepts

Table of Contents

Introduction

At 8:10 am on the morning of November 12, 1997 four US-based auditors from Union Texas Petroleum and their local driver were traveling west on Tamiz Ud Din Road in the Pakistani port city of Karachi when their vehicle was cut off by a red Honda Civic. Before they or their driver could react several armed men jumped from the Civic and began firing their Kalashnikov rifles into the auditors' vehicle. The unarmored Nissan station wagon was no protection against the hail of 7.62mm rounds and the four Americans and their Pakistani driver were killed instantly. While not the most recent incident of violence against Western travelers and admittedly one of the more extreme examples it nonetheless it illustrates a number of lessons that will be covered through the course of this book. Some of these key points – which also apply to other crimes like kidnappings and robberies - are:

- Time and place predictability give potential attackers an advantage and increase your vulnerability. In this case media reports at the time of the event stated that the auditors were picked up each day at their hotels at about 8:00 am and there was no variance to this routine or to the route that they took.
- These types of incidents frequently occur when the victim is in transit and in particular in and around vehicles.
- Travelers should be aware of the nature of criminal and terrorist threats and take reasonable measures to mitigate them. In this incident the methods used were similar to an attack that occurred to US consulate employees about two years previously.

Throughout the book we will be looking at various incidents and case studies that illustrate different aspects of personal security. In many of these cases there will be a discussion of mistakes that the victim made that frequently contributed to the outcome. It is critical to stress that our intent is not to blame the victim but rather to learn from the past mistakes of others and take that knowledge to develop better measures that we can apply ourselves to improve our own personal security in the future. This is better and more constructive than to take a fatalistic attitude to crime and violence and believe that it is unavoidable.

At the same time it is also important to highlight that there are no ironclad guarantees and that it is possible to do everything right and still be a victim. Also it is important to understand that the information provided here is intended as a resource and a guideline and its application will vary greatly from person-to-person, location-to-location and situation-to-situation. Unfortunately there are no black-and-white answers, no one-size-fits-all series of pat responses to every conceivable situation. There are however learning points that can be taken and applied to greatly enhance your personal security and safety. There are also elements that are not widely known by the general public but probably should be and also a number of myths that need to be dispelled and pitfalls that need to be identified.

Common Myths & Pitfalls

Common Myths

Myth #1: It can't happen to me.

This is perhaps less a myth and more a mindset. Crime victims, even those living in violent places with friends and relatives that have been victims of crime still sometimes hold on to the mindset that it can't happen to them. Not only does this usually mean the person has taken little or no proactive measures to protect themselves but it also significantly contributes to a delayed reaction time because the person is in a state of denial and when events begin to unfold they can't process what is happening and respond quickly enough.

Myth #2: If it does happen it was destined to happen or it was fate and there is nothing I can do about it.

This is the fatalistic attitude mentioned earlier. There is a phrase for it in Arabic: "Insh'Allah" --- if God wills it. While it's true that you can do everything right and still become a victim due to uncontrollable circumstances more often than not you can take significant measures to avoid or deter a problem or at a minimum recognize it more rapidly and take appropriate responsive action.

Myth #3: Victims are selected at random and most crime is spontaneous.

Victims are almost always selected and there is almost always some element of planning involved in any crime. Its true the victim selection and planning may occur very rapidly but it still occurs. The only really exception to this is situations involving civil unrest, rioting and other types of violence that occurs on a larger scale where particular victims may truly be in the wrong place at the wrong time.

Myth #4: Armed security or carrying weapons is always better than unarmed security.

This comes down to training whether it's the individual arming themselves or employing an armed security detail in a high threat environment or in response to a specific threat. Armed security definitely has its place and is appropriate under certain conditions. A person arming themselves but not getting training in how and when to employ their weapon in a tactical manner and under stress may actually increase their risk rather than reduce it. Likewise employing armed personnel who are not well trained and don't handle their weapons safely (as is often the case in the developing world) may also increase risk.

Myth #5: You should always comply with an attacker's demands.

While this is overwhelmingly true in the case of property crimes it is much more ambiguous and situational when it comes to any personal crime. If your assailant just wants your wallet or watch you should surrender it. If the assailant becomes physically abusive, tries to restrain you or tries to move you from the area then there are a number of factors that must be considered very rapidly and an individual decision must be made.

Myth #6: You should never let the attacker move you from the first crime scene.

This is also overwhelmingly true in the US and most of the developed world. The theory – which is fundamentally sound – is that if the crime is an economic crime the attacker will be satisfied with your property and will leave. If the attacker wants to move you to a place where he can control you – also known as crime scene two – then he likely intends to subject you to some type of torture or sadistic treatment and you are far better off resisting at crime scene one. In many developing countries where kidnap for ransom and express kidnapping are a regular occurrence it is not necessarily true. In those situations it may well be an economically motivated crime and you may have a better chance complying with the kidnappers and very likely being released upon the payment of a ransom or upon taking money out of an ATM machine in the case of an express kidnapping. There is no right answer for every situation and for every person. You need to look at crime trends in the environment you are in and make decisions based on the situation you find yourself in.

Myth #7: Local inhabitants know the security situation best and can give good guidance.

While local contacts are very valuable when gathering information about the security situation in the location where you are or will be traveling they should not be the sole source of this information and their input should not be accepted as gospel. Frequently locals do not know the security situation that well at all unless they are in a capacity where they deal with security issues or incidents regularly and often the information they have is anecdotal or based on gossip and urban myth. It's also important to consider that locals may have a very different threshold of what is normal or acceptable in terms of levels of crime, violence or terrorist threat. They may be accustomed to a level of violence, unrest or uncertainty in their society that is totally different from what you are used to. Also for cultural reasons or in some cases personal reasons (in particular when there is a business connection to the local contact) they may intentionally understate or misrepresent the threat level. Use local contacts and sources to gather information but view their input with a critical eye and in the context of information derived from other sources.

Myth #8: Most personal security is just common sense.
While it's fair to say that many personal security measures may appear obvious – common sense means different things to different people and arguably common sense is not all that common. There is also a lot to be studied and learned in terms of criminal practices and

methods that will enhance your security and goes beyond what is "common sense"

In addition to these myths there are a number of common pitfalls when it comes to personal security. By recognizing these pitfalls you can avoid them:

Pitfall #1: Using dated or overly anecdotal information to assess your destination.

The world is a dynamic place. When planning travel to a particular location it's important to use current information. Beirut today – while it has its security issues, some fairly significant – is not the Beirut of 1983 when the city was carved up by warring militias. At one time Abidjan, Cote D'Ivoire was considered the Paris of Africa but that is no longer the case. Caracas, Venezuela is much more dangerous today than it was even a few years ago.

Pitfall #2: Being too trusting of strangers.

Many travelers are much too accepting of approaches by strangers. While developing friendships with people in different countries is one of the great advantages of foreign travel it must be done judiciously and sensibly. When a stranger approaches you unfortunately there is sometimes an ulterior motive at work.

Pitfall #3: Being too trusting of local contacts

In addition to strangers, even local contacts should be treated with a degree of caution. Occasionally local contacts and partners will have a separate and hidden agenda. This doesn't mean that you should be rude to your local contacts or be excessively paranoid about them. It does mean that you should not follow them blindly or believe everything they say.

Pitfall #4: Believing your individual rights go with you when you travel overseas

For many of us living in western democracies we have come to accept our individual freedoms and rights as immutable and inalienable and as something that goes with us when we travel. This is a dangerous misconception. When you are in another country you are subject to the laws of that country which may be very, very different from your own.

Pitfall #5: Having too much confidence that your Embassy can assist you or solve all your problems.

The Embassy or Consulate is usually very limited in what they can do for you if you run afoul of local authorities. Typically this is confined to visiting you to check on your welfare and perhaps recommending or arranging for local legal representation.

Methodology

This book covers a variety of topics on personal and travel security beginning with situational awareness and basic individual protective measures. This section is perhaps the most important in the book as these really are the fundamental concepts that will help keep you safe whether at home or abroad. You should read these sections first and if you only read portions of the book you should definitely read these above all others.

Next the book outlines some of the key components of travel security breaking them down by stage from planning and air travel to arrival to transport to hotel and so forth. Then there are sections dealing with residential security, different types of crime, medical and evacuation planning and dealing with local contacts.

The skeleton of the book originally appeared on the Protective Concepts blog on Word Press and much of the book was pulled verbatim from the blog. The book is therefore a series of mini-articles on different topics. You can choose to either read the book cover-to-cover or by selecting the portions that are of interest or applicable to you.

The objective of this book is to go beyond what many other travel security books offer and which will hopefully give you a deeper understanding of functional ways to enhance your personal security. The book will be updated as necessary.

The methods discussed here are designed to be scalable. Everyone does not face the same level of risk. Some people might be specifically targeted, others are just working or traveling in a high risk area, some people may fall into both these categories. The degree of time invested and level of security measures taken will depend in large part on your level of risk,

Personal security is more art than science and it is also possible to do everything right and still be a victim. It is also very situationally driven and one works well for one person in one set of circumstances may not work well for another person. It's important as you read this book to think about your own thresholds and tolerances and also about the types of situations you are likely to find yourself in and how these concepts might be applied.

Situational Awareness

Situational awareness is the under-appreciated and in fact sometimes unappreciated element of personal security. Of all the things a person can do to keep themselves safe the most important and in fact most fundamental is to be aware of their surroundings and what is happening in their environment. This in conjunction with a basic understanding and ability to recognize potential threats is infinitesimally more important that any hard skill like shooting, martial arts/combatives or anything else.

Despite that awareness usually gets the short shrift. Discussions of personal security often give it only cursory mention or refer to it as "common sense" and don't take the time to emphasize how important it really is and how to best utilize and develop awareness. Look at how many books, DVDs and training seminars there are on combat shooting, physical self defense skills and the like and how much is available on the market dealing with awareness.

Security is often looked at as a purely functional skillset when in fact the most important aspects are mental. While I hesitate to throw out an unscientific percentage -- I think it is safe to say that a large number of personal crimes ranging from petty crimes like pickpocketing and purse snatching to violent confrontational crime like armed robbery and carjacking could have been avoided or at least mitigated if the victim was more aware in the moments leading up to the event.

In our multi-tasking world with an ever-increasing amount of distractions this issue of focused situational awareness has never been more important.

Cooper's Colors

No discussion of awareness would seem complete without a mention of Cooper's Colors. Originally publicly introduced and propagated by retired Marine Lieutenant Colonel Jeff Cooper. Cooper was the founder of American Pistol Institute, later called Gunsite and was an early proponent of combat handgunning. In his book *Principles of Personal Defense* Cooper outlined four levels of mindset:

White: Unaware and unprepared. In this condition you are unaware of your surroundings and unprepared to respond to a threat against you. Unfortunately many people walk around at this level everyday.

Yellow: Relaxed alert. You are aware of what is going on around you and you have mentally recognized that a threat may appear and you may need to respond to it. You are not however in a hyper-vigilant state. This is a relaxed state that can be maintained for long periods of time without fatigue. This is the level you should be in most of the time, in particular whenever you are in public.

Orange: Specific alert or heightened alert. You have identified a particular threat and have made the mental decision that you will act if the threat takes a certain action. This can also apply to entering a location or area where there is an increased threat that requires deliberate attention. This is not a relaxed state and cannot be effectively maintained for long periods of time.

Red: Condition Red is fight. This is pretty self explanatory. You are in a personal combat situation or a survival/self preservation mode.

Cooper's Colors and variations of it have been adopted by numerous entities, instructors and so forth, sometimes with minor modifications. Some also use a fifth condition call Condition Black that refers to a breakdown of mental and physical performance due to being overwhelmed by a situation – for example moving from condition white to red as the result of an ambush attack.

Many US Citizens may recognize this color scheme from the Department of Homeland Security's Threat Levels that were originally used and later abandoned in favor of the National Threat Advisory System. The color system arguably better relates to personal security measures than to national threat levels.

In my opinion the key points to take away are:

(1) Awareness levels are scalable.

(2) Condition Yellow is arguably the level we should all maintain most of the time.

(3) We will likely move back and forth between levels yellow and orange as we encounter different people and situations in our daily routine.

(4) There are some inherent dangers in Condition White. We should recognize Condition white and not use it when we are in public.

When to raise your level of awareness

Understanding where you are most likely to be attacked and knowing how to ratchet up your alertness level appropriately is a key component of personal protection -- probably the key component.

You can't walk around hyper-alert in condition orange all the time. You'll be exhausted and at some point - probably pretty quickly - it will become counterproductive.

Whether you are an at-risk person who may be specifically target for attack, kidnapping or some other crime for whatever reason or whether you are - like most of us - more likely to be the victim of an opportunistic crime you should recognize that you are more vulnerable and the likelihood is greater at certain locations and at certain times.

I'll exclude mentioning the more obvious places and times like late at night and in a bad neighborhood or secluded area -- although of course these are places and times that call for heightened vigilance.

Here are some of the times when you should avoid distraction and focus on your environment:

Arrivals and departures: whether you are leaving or arriving at your home, office, supermarket, gym, shopping mall, etc. you should take a moment to look around and observe the people and vehicles in the area and assess if anyone might present a threat to you. This is particularly true if you are entering or exiting a vehicle.

Boarding Mass Transportation: when stepping on to a subway car, bus or even an aircraft cabin you should look at your fellow travelers and assess which ones, if any might present a potential threat.

Areas where you are channelized or your options for maneuver or movements are restricted: These might be bridges, narrow roads with a blind curve, etc. Often referred to as chokepoints these are locations that are well suited for ambush-style attacks.

Identified Danger Areas: these are locations that have a past history of violent or criminal incidents occurring. In some overseas locations where civil unrest and rioting are practically the national pastime these can be focal points where crowds form or protests regularly occur.

The above list is far from exhaustive but should give you a good starting point.
When in these locations you should put away the Blackberry, the iPhone and whatever other distractions away, stop compiling the shopping list or planning your weekend and focus on the environment around you - in particular people or things that might cause you harm.

The Danger of Feeling "Safe"

Some cities feel dangerous. If you have ever been to Kinshasa or Lagos, Peshawar or Karachi you know what I mean. Abject poverty, streets packed with teeming masses eyeing you, the wealthy foreigner, hungrily. Many other cities don't feel that dangerous but are. Johannesburg, with its skyscrapers boasts a high violent crime rate and at one time held a record for sexual assaults. Its very easy to be lulled into complacency on the streets of Bogota with its crowds of smartly dressed business people and trendy restaurants and bars and easy to forget that this is the capital of a country that was until recently one of the leading countries for kidnapping in the world and a place that still has a healthy - or unhealthy - rate of street crime.

While the level of crime in Bogota and Johannesburg has improved both are still locations with real security concerns. Other cities like Buenos Aires can lull the visitor by making them feel like they are in Europe yet taxi crimes and express kidnappings occur fairly regularly. Sometimes the inherent feel we get in a particular city can be deceptive and misleading.

Noted personal security author and executive protection firm owner Gavin DeBecker has written much about the value of intuition (most notably in his book the Gift of Fear) in detecting dangerous situations and recognizing when a threat is present even when we can't quite articulate it. DeBecker is spot on when he notes our ability to subconsciously detect warning signs in our environment and the importance of heeding these warnings. Unfortunately the converse is often not true.

It can be very easy to fall into complacency - especially in what feels like a "familiar" environment or an environment we are conditioned to feel is low threat. If you are in an environment that is very alien to what you are used to you are likely to feel the threat more palpably. You are less likely to roam freely around the area. You will be more inclined to practice good security measures and limit your exposure. In such an environment there may also be less enticement to go out on the economy. In some of the cities we mentioned above you may feel very at ease. The location and the people may seem more familiar to you. There may be more to do. More opportunity to move around independently and also more exposure. This exposure may in fact be exacerbated by you dropping your guard. In the more austere and threatening location you are sometimes actually less exposed since you are more cognizant of the threat and not spending time on the local economy.

Therefore sometimes your vulnerability is greater in these cities that are more modern looking and more familiar. You are probably more likely to be walking around, going to restaurants and doing other activities that put you in much closer proximity to the local criminal element.

The best way to deal with this is to know the security situation in the location where you are going, the type of crimes that occur there and plan accordingly. You can still go out on the economy in these locations by practicing good situational awareness, avoiding potentially dangerous locations and situations and continually reminding yourself that the threat is present. This will help you combat the complacency that can leave you vulnerable.

Proactive Individual Protective Measures

Individual protective measures are the steps you take everyday to mitigate the risk of crime and violence. As mentioned earlier these are scalable measures depending both on the person's risk profile and the particular location or situation. Many of these measures can be relatively easily ingrained to the level that they do not require a great deal of conscious thought and become habit.

Time and Place Predictable

One of the main factors to reduce the likelihood of being a victim of a targeted attack is to not be time and place predictable. This is especially true for "at-risk" personnel who are more likely to be specifically targeted. What do I mean by at-risk personnel? These are people that because of their profile, actions, behavior, etc. are likely to be targets of violent crime for economic, political, personal or other reasons. Some examples might be:

Expatriates or long term business travelers living/working in a high crime or politically unstable area.

Politicians, activists, journalists or others that take a political position that may be at odds with people or groups prone to violence.

Stalking victims and victims of domestic violence.

People working in cash businesses or people working in business where they have access to unusually large amounts or money or valuables.

Celebrities and others that have a high public profile such as broadcast journalists.

Business people involved in disputes with partners, customers, suppliers, etc. This is particularly true in the developing world.

Witnesses in criminal cases.

Judges and lawyers depending on the type of cases they handle.

Government personnel such as diplomats or military personnel stationed abroad.

High net worth individuals

People who are at-risk or more prone to be the victim of a targeted crime should consider the role that time and place predictability plays in these types of incidents and take steps to reduce their vulnerability and mitigate the risk.

Most criminals, terrorists and other violent actors will conduct some type of surveillance to determine locations where there victim is both vulnerable to attack and predictable. The greater your predictability the easier you make it for this type of assailant.

For most people two locations are place predictable: home and work. For many people there may be others like the gym, a favorite restaurant or a favorite place to get coffee. For most people there are defined routes between home and work that are taken everyday or almost everyday and there are points on these routes - typically chokepoints - where they are particularly vulnerable to attack and where there are points of concealment and ready escape routes for the attacker or attackers.

By varying routes and departure and arrival times at-risk personnel can at least make it more difficult to attack them. We will discuss route analysis in greater depth separately.

Historically a large number of kidnappings and assassinations have occurred in the morning as the victim left their home. A classic example is the 1992 kidnapping of Exxon executive Sidney Reso which is often used as a case study. Reso was kidnapped by a former Exxon employee as he left his New Jersey home one morning.

Arguably most people are more predictable when leaving home in the morning. For most there is little opportunity for variance of route at this point as they can usually turn right or left and that's it. For this reason -- and because of these constraints one thing you can do is recognize this vulnerability and heighten your awareness when leaving your home as we discussed earlier.

People are creatures of habit. Often in the workplace even if an employee doesn't have an assigned parking space they generally park in the same area each day. Understanding these vulnerabilities and making a conscious effort to change them or at least heightening awareness at these key times is a critical element of a good personal security plan.

Does everyone need to focus on varying routes and times to not be predictable? I don't think they do. I think this is more important for people at risk like the examples mentioned above. I do think everyone benefits from recognizing these vulnerable points and times and raising their alertness level accordingly. Circumstances change and the person who may not need these measures today may be at risk tomorrow.

Surveillance Detection for Personal Security

Most attacks, robberies, kidnappings, sexual assaults and other forms of personal, confrontational crime occur after a period of observation and target selection. This can range from a period of weeks or months (or in rare cases even years) in the case of terrorist attacks to less than a minute or two in cases of a street robbery.

During this period the criminal or terrorist assesses and selects a target, determines periods of vulnerability on the part of the victim, identifies potential escape routes and considers potential obstacles to execution and escape. This is typically done by conducting surveillance even if that surveillance is very rudimentary and in some cases very compressed.

This process is in place to a greater or lesser extent in virtually every case where a victim is targeted (exceptions would be more random violence resulting from civil unrest, etc. and incidents where the victim is accidental or collateral damage).

For certain types of events there will be a longer lead time and therefore a greater opportunity to detect surveillance or other pre-operational indicators. In other cases it may be very compressed but by understanding the concepts you can apply many of the same techniques to detect it and prevent the attack from occurring or at least better defend yourself should you not be able to avoid the event.

Understanding basic surveillance detection principles can go a long way towards keeping you safe.

When using surveillance detection principles as part of your personal security program there are two levels that can be used: passive and active. In an active program you would design an implement surveillance detection routes (SDR) that include preplanned stops and movements designed to cause anyone that might be following you to inadvertently expose themselves. This requires a level of training and practice and is probably not necessary for most people most of the time.

The second method is passive surveillance detection which can be done very simply. It does require a level of focus and awareness but with a little practice this can become a habit.

Three of the key components to watch for are:

Time and Distance: Seeing the same person, people or vehicles over time and distance. For example if you see the same person at the airport, then later at you hotel and then at the restaurant where you are having dinner it could be simply coincidence or it could be a cause for concern. The greater the frequency and the greater the number of sightings the higher the level of concern that you might be under observation.

Correlating Actions: Watch for people and vehicles whose movement appears to correlate with yours. An example would be when departing your house you pull out into the street in your vehicle and a car that has been parked up the street pulls out into traffic behind you. Things to watch for are: people who either move or seem to take notice when you move or arrive/depart at a location.

Out of place: Watch for people whose appearance and or behavior appears incongruous with the environment they are in.

With the exception of national intelligence and security services and some sophisticated terrorist organizations most surveillants are going to have a very rudimentary skillset and limited resources. When they succeed more often than not it's because many if not most people walk around all day in a distracted, unaware state of mind. Understanding these simple principles, applying them and being alert will go a long way to keeping you safer.

Blending in & the Gray Man

For Westerners and Americans in particular our ability to blend in will be very dependent on the society we are in. In many cases we may not really be able to blend in but we can avoid unnecessarily standing out. This means leaving the cowboy hats, sports jerseys, Oakley sunglasses, etc. at home. Likewise the t-shirts with American flags and patriotic slogans.

To truly blend in is difficult -- even if you are the same race or ethnicity as the host population. In the Philippines as an example, native Filipinos can usually readily identify Balikbayan - Filipinos who have lived abroad for years and then returned to the Philippines. These Balikbayan are often targeted for robbery due to their perceived affluence.

Interestingly I have heard - but cannot verify - that in Northern Ireland Catholics and Protestants can distinguish each other on the street by appearance.

Therefore the goal of truly blending in may be out of reach in many cases. Its probably better to be the "gray man" and do nothing and wear nothing that will unduly draw attention to yourself or invite interest.

You should be free of any obvious national or political indentifiers, not wear conspicuous jewelry or clothing, not appear too rich or too poor, etc. While you might not want to look like a high profile businessman you also might not want to appear like a backpacker either.

Contrary to popular perception, backpackers and similar low budget travelers are targeted for crimes regularly. This is in part because they are frequently carrying all their money and other valuables with them all the time and may actually be carrying more cash than the rich businessman who is relying on credit cards and local representatives to cover his expenses.

Additionally, backpackers and other poorly dressed travelers may draw unwanted attention from the local police and security forces not to mention immigration and customs personnel at the airport. This is especially true in developing countries.

Therefore the best approach may be the middle ground. Not too rich, not too poor. Not clearly identifiable as any particular nationality. While the gray man (or gray woman) may not truly blend in - he or she may draw the least amount of attention and sometimes that is the best you can do.

Sanitize Yourself for Travel

You don't need to cut the tags out of your clothes but before traveling abroad its important to think about things that you are carrying, either on your person, in your bags or electronically in your devices that may cause trouble for you with foreign authorities. In the earlier section on being the gray man and blending in we discussed clothing. This time we will focus more on the types of things that you might be carrying that may cause unnecessary problems. I am not suggesting that you never carry these types of things when you travel - only that you give it some consideration in the context of your trip.

Here are some categories to consider:

Military or government ID. If you are a reservist, a government contractor or otherwise have some type of government ID you may want to leave it at home if you are traveling on private sector business. Obviously this doesn't apply if you are going to need the ID on your trip.

Reading material, videos and other media that might be considered offensive in the country you are traveling to. This is particularly true in some of the more conservative Islamic countries.

Military style clothing such as camouflage or 5.11 clothing. In many developing nations police and military authorities tend to view military clothing negatively and may not understand that you are wearing it for durability, comfort, etc.

Police or military paraphernalia such as body armor, handcuffs, batons, magazines, shell casings, etc. Even countries like United Arab Emirates have issues with this and have detained travelers with this sort of gear in their luggage.

Political material and media that may be offensive to the host government or contrary to its policies.

Satellite phones and GPS units. These are viewed with suspicion - and in some places are outright illegal - particularly in countries with a history of coups, political instability or foreign intervention.

Computers and other devices with encryption software loaded on them. In some countries this is illegal and in some others while legal it may draw unnecessary scrutiny.

Sensitive company information. It goes without saying that you should limit the amount of proprietary information you carry with you when traveling abroad. Foreign governments can and sometimes will gain access to this information if they choose to examine your computer and other devices as part of a security or customs check on arrival or departure. In some cases they may also surreptitiously access it during your stay.

Sensitive personal information. You want to be cautious about carrying sensitive personal information like banking and financial information, personal contact information and the like that may be compromised.

Medications. Be aware of what medications can be legally carrier into your destination and any restrictions that may exist such as the need for a prescription, prior approval from the host country Ministry of Health, etc.

Passport Stamps and Visas. The classic example is the presence of an Israeli stamp in your passport barring you from entry in some Arab and Muslim countries. If you have passport entries that might be problematic at your destination country then consider getting a new passport in advance. Do NOT tear pages or visas out of your passport. This is a crime many places and will cause you serious problems if detected.

The above guidelines are very situationally dependent -- they are going to vary widely from country-to-country and situation-to-situation. I don't want to appear to be saying you need to follow these for every trip. They are however things to consider, especially if travel takes you to places where the government closely scrutinizes visitors.

Personal Risk Assessment

Considering that personal and travel security rely heavily on context its important to consider how the threat relates to you whether at home or abroad. Understanding this contextual relationship lets you realistically determine how much effort, energy and possibly money you should invest in your security.

The best way to do this is to conduct a personal risk assessment. This can be done yourself or you can hire a consultant to do it for you and it can be as detailed as you want to make it. If you do it yourself its important to be as brutally honest with yourself as you can for the assessment to be accurate and have value. This assessment can be done from a lifestyle perspective for an at-risk person or a person living in a high-risk area or it can be done for a particular event like an overseas business trip. It can also be done using qualitative or quantitative methods or a combination of the two. Most people will be more likely to use qualitative means.

The standard formula for a risk assessment is that Risk equals Threat x Vulnerability. For our purposes this means you need to begin by identifying a threat or threats that exist and then look at vulnerabilities in their schedule, routine or lifestyle where their exposure to this threat is increased.

As an example a businessman traveling to a two-day meeting in Johannesburg might identify threats such as carjacking and armed robbery. In particular he may look at the practice of criminals following people from the airport and robbing them en route or at their destination. He might also consider the high level of gratuitous violence often involved in these crimes. On a review of his itinerary he notes that the meetings will all be held at a 5-star hotel adjacent to the airport terminal and that he will be staying at the same hotel. In this case the threat level is high but his vulnerability is low so the risk is relatively low.

Another aspect to consider is the probability vs. criticality or impact. Some events are more likely but the consequences are not too severe. Others are less likely but the consequences may be devastating. Two examples to look at:

A photographer is going on an assignment in Barcelona that will involve a lot of work in public venues. The threat of pickpocketing and petty crime may be high but the criticality of these types of incidents is relatively low -- unless of course his cameras are stolen and he can't complete the job. On the other hand an engineer has a 2-week assignment in Islamabad, Pakistan. He will be staying at a western brand hotel that has been previously attacked with a massive vehicle bomb. Hotels of this type are targeted for spectacular attacks by militant groups. In this case the relative probability that the hotel will be attacked while he is there is relatively low. However based on past incidents if the hotel is attacked the impact is likely to be severe.

Using this information you can determine the level of risk you face - either daily or for a specific activity or event as well as the likelihood and potential impact of an event occurring. Using this information you can determine what countermeasures if any you should implement to mitigate the risk.

When conducting your personal risk assessment you should consider the types of threats that exist and factors we have discussed such as time and place predictability, modes of transportation, type of accommodation/lodging and so forth. You should also implement the adversarial view so you can see yourself through the eyes of a potential assailant.

4 Steps to Taking the Adversary's Perspective and Enhancing Your Security

When you are evaluating your own personal security its very useful to take the perspective of your adversary -- for most of us that is the common criminal but depending on your location it may also include terrorists, militants, members of organized criminal groups or others. Traditionally most people and most organizations have viewed their security from the inside looking out. However it might be better to look at it from the outside in - the same way a predator looks at it.

Here is a four-step process you can use:

(1) Consider your attractiveness as a target. Are you well-known,

wealthy or perceived as wealthy, politically active, involved in a business dispute or is there another reason you might be specifically targeted? Beyond that are you someone who is likely to be targeted in a crime of opportunity due to your physical appearance? In 1984 Betty Grayson and Morris Stein published a now-famous study about physical signals that potential victims unwittingly send to their assailants. The Grayson Stein study involved videotaping pedestrians on the streets of New York City and then subsequently showing the videos to inmates incarcerated for violent assaults. The inmates were split into different groups and told to rate the people videotaped on a scale of 1 to 10 with one being the most attractive target and 10 the least. The inmates responses were shockingly consistent with regard to who the most attractive victims were.

On further review Grayson and Stein determined that the more likely victims differed in stride, fluidity of movements, head position, etc from those who were deemed the toughest targets and not desirable. While these nonverbal cues may not be characteristics that can be readily changed - just being aware of them will be an asset in protecting yourself.

(2) Aggressor Tactics, Techniques and Procedures and Modus Operandi. After considering your attractiveness or likelihood as a potential target you should consider the methods a potential attacker might use. Look at what type of tactics are common in the area where you live or work. Consider common carjacking techniques in use in Nairobi. This is a good example to use. Many carjackings and armed robberies in Nairobi have occurred when the victim drove up to the vehicle gate at their home. While they are waiting for the gate to be opened another vehicle - which has either been following them or parked nearby observing their residence -- will pull up and block them in. The assailants will deploy from the vehicle and rob their victim. Understanding the tactics used by criminals and threat groups in your area of operation is a critical component of this process. In a broader sense it's helpful to know that targeted attacks - both assassinations and kidnappings frequently occur in the morning as the victim is leaving their residence. This is largely true worldwide. One if the more notable examples is the kidnapping of Exxon executive Sidney Reso as he left his New Jersey home in

1992.

(3) Develop a predatory mindset. This is anethmatic to most people but its one of the best ways to understand how criminals and other hostile people and groups view the world. To gain an understanding of this do a simple mental exercise: the next time you are in a public place such as a shopping district, mall, etc. try to identify people who would be good victims to assault and rob. By the way - this is not an original idea. Many instructors and writers on this topic have advocated the same exercise for the same reason. The one who comes most readily to mind is Rory Miller but there are several others as well. Once you have identified likely victims think how you would isolate and attack them in a way that would give you the best chance of success and the ability to escape. Don't take notes -- this is a mental exercise. By doing this occasionally - and in conjunction with your knowledge of assailant tactics - you will develop a greater appreciation for the adversary's perspective and the steps he will take in selecting a victim and carrying out an attack.

(4) Look at yourself and your routine through the adversary's eyes. Where are you vulnerable in your day-to-day life? Where are you time and place predictable? Where and when are you likely to be distracted or unaware? Where on your routes are likely attack sites? Ask yourself these questions and try to view yourself through the adversary's perspective. Once you begin to answer these you can develop countermeasures to make yourself a harder target.

Using Dummy Wallets

Dummy or throwaway wallets should be a consideration when traveling abroad. Carrying an old wallet with some cash - enough to pacify a local criminal (for most locations probably $20 to $60 USD) gives you the option of surrendering this wallet and some cash without risking losing everything. Ideally you should put some other paper in the wallet such as receipts but avoid having any documents with your personal information that could be used to track or locate you.

If confronted in a robbery situation you can surrender the throwaway wallet and the criminal will likely want to take it and get away as rapidly as possible allowing you to avoid losing your real valuables.

Even if you don't use a dummy wallet another good strategy is to divide your money, credit cards and other valuables among different places so that a theft will hopefully only result in the loss of some of it and not everything.

Be cautious about securing anything valuable in the safe in the hotel room. Staff can access the safe and its the first place someone will look. Additionally there are methods for defeating hotel room safes. In some locations the main safe in the hotel might be an option if you get a receipt as the hotel has some accountability. In some places even the hotel safe isn't a good option and alerting the staff you have valuables may increase your risk of being targeted.

Its best to leave unnecessary valuables at home and things you must bring like cash and credit cards can be dispersed in different locations on your person and in your belongings. You can also consider putting some of it in a money belt or in specially designed security containers that are designed to look like other common objects (shaving cream cans, etc.). The effectiveness of these security containers is debatable and they vary in terms of quality but they are an option. Padlocked bags may provide some deterrent but any softsided luggage can be breached at the zipper with a cheap ballpoint pen and usually subsequently closed without leaving a trace of the intrusion. Anyone given sufficient time to search will likely find where your things are stashed but many times the thief may not have the luxury of time.

To Resist or Not to Resist -- That is the Question

One question that often comes up is whether or when to resist a criminal. There is no clear-cut answer as it depends a lot on the situation and the individual involved. Generally though most people agree that pure property or economically motivated crimes should not be resisted. If the criminal just wants your money or jewelry or whatever property you have it's best to turn it over without delay. You should never put your life at risk for property. In many places in the world criminals are armed and will use violence at the slightest provocation.

If the criminal is a violent physical crime against your person such as an assault, attempted rape, etc. the response is really a personal decision: what will you tolerate or not tolerate? Again it will usually be driven by the situation as well.

An area that may be less clear is an abduction or kidnapping. In these situations its important to know the local norms and the local security environment. In the US for example kidnapping for ransom is relatively rare. Many abductions are done by sexual predators or others that will do you harm regardless. For this reason many experts recommend fighting back to prevent being moved to what is referred to as crime scene 2. The abduction site is crime scene 1 and its probably better to resist at crime scene 1 than risk being taken to crime scene 2 where the predator will have more time and better control over you and the consequences may be much worse. However when you shift this dynamic overseas the scenario may change dramatically. In many international locations kidnap-for-ransom is rampant and in many of these places kidnap victims are usually released unharmed. In Colombia as an example, there was a period when kidnapping was a very developed business and kidnappers generally kept their victims alive and managed their captivity well to be able to collect the ransom. In some locations such as Yemen and Egypt's Sinai Peninsula foreigners are kidnapped by local tribes as a bargaining tool in disputes with the government. In these cases the victims are usually released unharmed after a short period. In many locations where express kidnapping is common victims are kept for a few hours to drain their ATM accounts and then they are released. Therefore it is reasonable to say there may be some abduction scenarios where not resisting increases the likelihood of a better outcome.

A similar - and often related issue to the abduction/kidnapping scenario is the risk of being tied up. If there is a home invasion at your residence or if you in a place of business when it is robbed and the perpetrators want to tied you up or otherwise restrain you should you resist? In some cases the criminals may want to do this simply for their own protection or to buy them more time to escape and they may mean you no harm. Of course you have no way of knowing their intention and some experts will correctly advise you not to trust what they tell you. Keep in mind that anytime you allow yourself to be restrained you reduce and probably remove your ability to fight back. That's a fairly significant consideration and something to think about before the incident occurs.

If you are the victim of an abduction or kidnapping chances are the perpetrator or perpetrators have done some planning and have chosen the time and place to attack so that circumstances favor them. It's also possible, in fact likely that they have committed this crime before. Also - the actual point of abduction is the most volatile time in a kidnapping. The criminals are on edge and worried about facing resistance so tensions are running high. That said it may still present the best opportunity to escape as once they have control over you they will move you to a location where they plan to confine you and the level of control will be even greater. At that point escape will likely be very difficult.

If you are fairly confused at this point or more confused than before you started reading that is normal. Like so many personal security questions there is no one right pat answer, no on-size-fits-all solution. There are only ideas and options to consider. You need to think about the environment you are in, your personal triggers, thresholds and tolerances and weigh the different options. Some thought should be given to these things before an incident ever occurs.

Considerations for Combatives

While we have focused continually on awareness and avoidance as a means to prevent becoming engaged in a physical conflict there may be times when it's unavoidable - especially to protect oneself from violence. While physical self defense measures our not our focus there is so much inaccurate, misleading or false information out there -- often delivered by people with good intentions -- that its important to at least discuss some general principles and concepts that will allow the reader to better distinguish useful and worthwhile training from training which is not so good or not so applicable

Some things to consider at the outset:

As we have discussed before, the criminal will attack at a time and place of his choosing where conditions favor him.

There will likely be weapons, multiple attackers or both involved. Some statistics on violence contradict this but they normally include "social violence" such as fistfights in bars and domestic incidents which are not our focus here.

The criminal will likely have committed this type of attack before and will have a game plan that has worked in the past.

If we are forced to counter this physically we must utilize the element of surprise, as much violence as possible and seek to disable the attacker enough to provide an opportunity to escape.

This means we need to utilize:

The element of surprise and non-telegraphic movement to the extent possible.

Gross motor attacks. Fine motor techniques and overly complex techniques will likely not be effective.

Repetitive attacks until the assailant is disabled or breaks contact and retreats.

Attacks to vulnerable soft tissue areas such as the eyes and throat that will inflict the maximum damage.

Use of palm strikes, hammer fists, rakes, elbows, knees and other tools that allow us to inflict damage without inadvertently injuring ourselves in the process.

Improvised weapons when available and applicable. A realistic consideration of how commonly carried items or accessible items can be effectively utilized as weapons and subsequent training in their use is necessary.

Perhaps the most important aspect is mindset and the willingness to use violence and inflict damage when necessary to protect yourself or others. It is however important to get some level of training in effective methods. The degree to which you train will largely be determined by your level of interest and ideally by your level of need. It can be difficult to find quality training that focuses on realistically dealing with violence. Its important to consider some of the points outlined above when selecting an instructor or school. Even after selecting an instructor and beginning training its important to have a critical mind and not accept everything at face value, be able to distinguish what is likely to work best for you and concentrate on realistic application under pressure and stress.

OPSEC & PERSEC Measures to Enhance Your Personal Security

Social Networks and the Threat to Personal Security

Recent open source reporting indicates that the Colombian National Police just arrested a group of criminals that were using Facebook to identify, profile and target victims for kidnapping. Initial reports the gang were using false Facebook profiles with pictures of beautiful women to target wealthy men as victims. They would use information in the victim's profile to assist them is selecting potential targets. They would then engage the target in online discussions to build report and elicit additional information. After a period of time, usually a few weeks they would arrange to meet the victim. When the victim arrived at the pre-arranged meeting location he would be drugged - most likely with scopolamine - and moved to another location where they would be tortured and held for ransom.

This incident not only illustrates the vulnerability of revealing too much information about yourself in social network websites and to unknown persons online but also touches on the use of drugs (probably Scopolamine in this case) in facilitating kidnaps and also the process of victim selection, use of honey traps and utilizing technology to do a valuation of potential targets.

The Facebook kidnapping gang is a clear example of what can go wrong if too much information is available in the public domain. Even information that is can only be viewed by friends or contacts can compromise you if you "friend" or "link" to people you don't know or don't know well.

Social networking is a key part of most of our lives now and most people use if for personal or professional reasons or both. The issue is not whether or not to use social networking but how to understand the vulnerabilities that exist and manage the type and amount of information available.

Social networks and the easy availability of online personal information is a huge force multiplier for stalkers, burglars, fraudsters, identity thieves, social engineers of all types, terrorists and kidnappers make it much quicker, easier and safer to compile detailed dossiers on potential victims and exploit that information to their advantage. Social networks also provide a vehicle to do a "cold approach" to a potential victim, establish rapport, gain additional information and arrange a physical meeting in person if desired. That appears to be what occurred in this case in Colombia.

It also significantly reduces the need for physical surveillance of the target and the vulnerability to exposure that exists with that activity. If the victim can be induced to voluntarily present themselves at a place and time of the criminal's choosing it makes it much easier to carry out the kidnapping with limited risk.

The lesson here is not to eliminate the use of social networks which would be unrealistic given the role they now play in society. The objective should be to understand the vulnerabilities that exist - especially in the context of your personal situation and risk profile. Arguably a soccer mom from Annapolis, Maryland and a wealthy Colombian businessman have very different risk profiles and would need to manage their personal information differently. While the soccer mom still has some level of risk, barring exceptional conditions (such as a stalking situation) her risk profile is much lower than the Colombian businessman.

Some things to consider regarding personal security when using social networks:

Security settings: most social networking platforms provide security settings that allow you to limit who is able to see what information about you and your personal network. Consider using these rather than the default settings.

Posting Potentially Compromising Information: Not only can posting information about your drunken weekend put you in a precarious position with your employer, clients, etc. it also provides insight into your personal lifestyle that can be exploited.

The risk of using applications like TripIt when linked to social networks that share your travel itinerary. This allows others to see where and when you are traveling.

The risk of using Foursquare and other GPS related applications that use your smartphone to identify and post your location to people in your social network.

Posting Photos: Posting a portrait photo of yourself gives a potential assailant who has never seen you before the ability to recognize you. Additionally many smartphone cameras also automatically geotag photos without the user being aware of it. When the photo is posted it is possible to retrieve the geotag to determine where the photo was taken.

Social networking is here to stay and its role in our personal and professional lives will only grow. There are numerous positive aspects of social media and it can be leveraged to your benefit in many ways.

It's important to look at the potential impact to your personal security based on an honest assessment of your personal risk profile. You should consider limiting what you post, who you allowed into your social network or in some cases both depending on your situation.

Social Engineering: Implications for your Security

Social engineering - the calculated manipulation and exploitation of people has historically been associated with cyber security issues. Computer hackers found they could best get access to secure networks by targeting the weakest link - the human factor.

The same techniques used to get an employee to give up their password or provide other information to facilitate entry into a network can be used to gather information to compromise a person's personal security as well.

Social engineering can use any one of a combination of several vectors to approach the target - telephone, email and in person being the three primary ones.

The example of the Colombian kidnapping gang that use Facebook to target their victims that we discussed is applicable here. While there is limited information currently available on that incident it appears the victims were cultivated over a period of weeks or months via the use of social engineering techniques on Facebook. The information available on Facebook gave the kidnap gang a foundation with which to build their approach. Knowing something about their victim - his lifestyle, interests and hobbies would help them develop an online relationship and build rapport that would put him at ease.

Understanding and recognizing the techniques employed in social engineering is the best defense against them. Here are some of the primary ones you may encounter:

Elicitation: Elicitation is a method of extracting information from an unwitting person by framing questions and statements in such a way that the person gives more information than they normally would or would intend to.

Pretexting: The social engineer presents himself as someone other than who he really is in order to get information or drive a certain course of action. In some cases this may mean the social engineer portrays himself as an authority figure. In the case of the Facebook Kidnap Gang the kidnappers presented themselves as beautiful, available young women. The anonymity of the Internet facilitates this immensely.

Influence and Persuasion Techniques: By artfully exploiting human desires to be liked, reciprocity and obligation and the introduction of fear social engineers can compel people to reveal sensitive information or perform a certain action on their behalf.

This is a broad overview of social engineering - in particular how it relates to personal security. Using clever techniques criminals can not only commit fraud and information theft, they can also facilitate violent crimes like kidnapping. These tactics may be directed at the victim himself/ herself or at unwitting third parties like coworkers and domestic staff. The first step to countering these techniques is being able to recognize them.

Loose Lips --- Recognizing and Avoiding Elicitation

In discussing social engineering and threats to your personal security we mentioned elicitation. Elicitation is a technique that is used by an adversary to get a person to unintentionally divulge more information about a particular subject than they normally would. It's used to gather confidential or proprietary information and in the realm of personal security it can be used by an adversary to gather information for use in targeting you or to build rapport with you or someone close to you.

While we are not going to attempt to teach elicitation or counter-elicitation here we are going top briefly outline some of the common techniques that are used so that you can recognize them being used against you. Remember these can be employed in person, over the phone or through electronic communication of various types such as email, online chat, etc.

This is by no means an exhaustive list but these are some of the key elicitation techniques you may encounter:

Flattery: The adversary will complement you on personal and or professional aspects of your life to build rapport and increase your likelihood to talk openly. This may include requests for advice based on your "expertise", etc.

False Statements: The adversary may make statements he or she knows are incorrect in order to prompt you to correct them by providing the correct information.

Provocative Statements: Similar to the false statement the adversary may make a statement that he or she knows will initiate an emotional response on your part and a desire to either strongly agree or disagree with them.

Disbelief: The adversary will feign disbelief at a statement you make to prompt you to elaborate more fully.

Naïveté: Similar to disbelief the adversary will feign ignorance to get you to "educate" him or her.

Quid pro Quo: The adversary may volunteer some innocuous or more likely false information about themselves so that by social convention you feel compelled to reveal something to them.

These are just some techniques may be used to get information about your schedule, your security profile, your business dealings, you personal wealth, your employer and so on. By recognizing when you might be encountering them you can make a conscious decision to reduce the amount of information you provide or break off the conversation.

While some of these are relatively sophisticated methods they have been and may be employed by foreign intelligence agencies and internal security units, organized crime groups, terrorists and others. Keep in mind as well that they may be aimed not only at you directly but also at your employees, associates, domestic staff, etc. Its important to train these people -- even if its just at a very rudimentary level -- to be cautious about people asking questions or try to get them to divulge information about you or your activities.

Unsolicited Approaches

In keeping with the themes of social engineering and elicitation it's a good point to discuss the need to be wary of unsolicited approaches. We also need to be mindful that these approaches are not necessarily made in person although they can be. In today's technological world they are frequently also made via email or through social media.

These types of unsolicited approaches are made by criminals and other dangerous people for a variety of reasons. Their objective is often fraud or theft of proprietary or classified information or other sensitive data. Sometimes - as we saw in the case of the Colombian Facebook kidnapping gang it can be to facilitate more violent crimes such as kidnapping, armed robbery or rape. Anytime people you don't know seek you out - whether in person or online - you should look at the situation with a critical eye and question their motivation.

I once attended a counterintelligence presentation that addressed this issue. The instructor - a short, overweight middle-aged man with a beard and glasses wearing suspenders and a bowtie - stepped to the podium. He began by saying how when he was at home in the US he couldn't get an attractive woman to give him the time of day or to even spit on his shoes. But when he goes overseas it's another story. He turns into Brad Pitt and beautiful women at the bar flock around him. He gets phone calls from women and has them knocking on his hotel room door at all hours of the night.

The point is well made. If these types of things don't happen to you regularly at home why are they suddenly happening when you arrive in country X? His presentation was focused on counterintelligence but the same techniques can be used even when the motivation may be different and is probably related to separating you from your money in some way. The broader concept is that you should be cautious of someone's potential ulterior motives if you are approached unexpectedly.

Sometimes these are "cold approaches" that come largely out of the blue and some are "warm approaches" where the person may have gathered some basic information on you (often through social media or other Internet resources) and has - or purports to have - something either professional or personal in common with you. This is one of the risks of posting too much on social media sites, especially concerning hobbies, interests and other things that can be used as a vehicle to get in contact with you, establish rapport and so forth.

These warm approaches can take place over time and may be very effective in getting you to gradually lower you guard. It appears that was the case in the Colombia Facebook case. The kidnap gang was apparently successful in convincing their wealthy male victims via Facebook that they were attractive women and by cultivating an online discussion and ultimately enticing them to come to a physical meeting where they were subsequently drugged and kidnapped.

There can also be "cold approaches" where you are approached by a stranger who initiates conversation without any prior connection of any sort.

Be wary - but not paranoid - if you are approached by a stranger. Always look at the situation with a critical mind and ask yourself what ulterior motives or hidden agendas might exist. You do not need to be rude but be cautious, especially if the situation seems unusual or outside your usual frame of reference.

The Criminal "Interview"

While we are discussing unsolicited approaches it's a good time to mention the criminal "interview" that is often the precursor to a robbery or assault. The interview occurs when the criminal engages the potential victim in conversation prior to initiating a crime. This usually serves two purposes (1) it gives the criminal or criminals and opportunity to further assess the suitability of their target and (2) it can serve as a distraction technique to get the potential victim to lower their guard and/or diver their attention which facilitates the attack.

The criminal usually interviews you by approaching you and asking a question - it may be for directions, the time of day or something similar. They will use this opportunity to gauge your reaction and your alertness level. Did they surprise you with their question? Did you jump back? Did you look down to consult your watch? Did you appear fearful and shrink back? All these factors will be processed in a second or two and he will make a determination whether or not to try to victimize you. Predatory criminals generally want to maximize their chances of committing their crime successfully, avoiding injury and getting away without being caught. They will usually factor this in when selecting a victim.

By demonstrating that you are alert and displaying a confident demeanor you reduce the chances that you will be selected for victimization. Notice I said "confident" and not "challenging". You do not want to appear so confident or aggressive that the criminal feels you are challenging him, especially if he is in a group in which case he may feel the need to prove himself to save face.

Ideally you want to be practicing good situational awareness and spot the potential criminal before he approaches you and be ready. Ensure you allow sufficient physical space between yourself and the other person. Also be mindful of possible accomplices in the area so that one is not able to come up behind you while you are focused on the primary threat. Do not allow yourself to be distracted by the question or request. As with our discussion of surveillance detection principles watch for correlating movement or signs that seemingly unconnected people are communicating with each other. Someone crossing a street at a diagonal in your direction or otherwise intentionally moving to cross or block your path should be an immediate warning sign.

Sometimes these approaches are innocent and the person really does want directions, to know what time it is or a light for their cigarette. Nonetheless you should be aware of these ruses and raise your alert level -- without over reacting -- when approached by someone you don't know.

Air Travel Security

While air travel in much of the world is typically very safe – and the statistically higher frequency of vehicular accidents as opposed to aviation accidents is often cited in making this point – there are definitely some risks involved, particularly in the developing world. The absence of regulatory enforcement, costs constraints and a lax safety culture can all contribute to raising the risk.

There are several key steps you can take to greatly enhance your safety and security when traveling by air:

Air carrier selection: Make every effort to select an airline with a good safety record. This may mean a longer or more costly trip but it's still worthwhile.

Avoid trouble spots: avoid changing flights in cities with serious safety concerns. A flight delay or cancellation could force you to remain overnight will little preparation or knowledge of the local threat environment.

Carry essential items on board in your carry-on bag. Don't put valuables or items that are critical for your trip in checked baggage. Checked baggage may be lost or stolen or items may be pilfered from inside the bag.

At the airport clear the security checkpoint as quickly as possible and remain in the "secure" side of the airport that is for screened and ticketed passengers until its time for your flight. Public areas of the airport are very vulnerable and as aviation and airport security increases there is likely to be a target shift to softer, easier access areas of the airport. This was evidenced in the recent bombing at the baggage claim area in Domodedovo Airport in Moscow.

When boarding the aircraft immediately locate the exits closest to you and determine the number of seats between you and the exit to ensure you can find it in periods of reduced visibility.

Assess your fellow passengers as they board and identify persons who might be a potential problem. This does not only mean potential terrorist concerns. Intoxicated passengers and air rage incidents are far more common.

Consider keeping valuables with you or in a bag under the seat in front of you as there have been issues with theft from bags in overhead bins, especially on long haul flights.

You may also want to place bags in the overhead bin opposite and forward of your seat to be able to observe them better.

Arrival

One of the most vulnerable points in international travel is arrival at a foreign airport and subsequent movement to your accommodation or first meeting. You are more likely than not going to be tired and a little disoriented and if it is your first visit to the particular city you will need to navigate the formalities such as passport control, perhaps reclaim your checked baggage and find your transportation. Perhaps dealing with a language barrier while you are doing this.

Criminals know you are vulnerable at this point and therefore lurk in and around airports waiting to prey on unsuspecting travelers. This may take the form of petty theft of baggage, pickpocketing or fraudulent taxi services where you are grossly over-charged to more violent and dangerous types of crime like kidnapping and armed robbery.

To limit your risk consider packing lightly whenever possible and avoiding checked bags - or at least multiple checked bags if possible. The more encumbered you are the more likely you will be to be distracted and therefore a more attractive a target you will be.

It goes without saying that the more you are able to rest or sleep on your flight -- especially if its a long flight -- the more rested and refreshed and therefore more aware you are likely to be.

A critical component of staying safe during the arrival process is selecting your ground transportation. Prior to departing you should research options for ground transportation at your destination and determine what is best and most appropriate for you. These options may run the full spectrum from public transportation to a close protection detail depending on the location and the specific circumstances.

In some Western European cities such as Paris, London and Amsterdam - there are reasonably efficient train services that will take you directly from the airport to the center of the city. These can be used safely provided you take reasonable measures to guard against pickpockets and other petty criminals.

In most locations the best option is usually to be met at the airport by a trusted local contact if you have one. If this is not possible then the next best option is to use prearranged transportation. This can be composed of anything from a car service or limo service to a close protection detail depending on the threat level of the location and the nature of the visit. When using prearranged transportation you should develop identification protocols in advance. You may want to not use your name or company name on the sign and instead have the driver use a predetermined alpha-numeric or other identifier. When possible at higher risk locations its good to try to get a photo of the driver in advance. Upon meeting the driver on arrival you may also want to ask for his identification or ask him questions to determine he is in fact your assigned driver. You should also have a contingency plan in mind in case you cannot find the driver.

Another less desirable option is to take a taxi. In mid-to-high threat locations taxis should generally be avoided due to the prevalence of taxi crime. When they must be taken it is strongly recommended to use a taxi stand at the terminal and not hail a taxi or accept an offer from touts who may be soliciting passengers in the terminal. In some airports there are prepaid taxi kiosks where you can arrange a taxi and prepay for your journey. If this option is not available and a taxi must be used then check with an information booth, taxi dispatcher or other source in the airport and get an idea of approximate cost for your trip and then verify the cost with the driver.

Transportation

Taxi Crime

Taking taxis in many countries is an activity fraught with risks. In most locations the safest option if you need to use taxis as opposed to dedicated prearranged transport is to use a radio-call taxi or a taxi set-up by a hotel or restaurant. Getting into taxis on the street can open you up to everything from minor theft - such as over-charging to serious, potentially violent crime.

A common modus operandi in many cities around the world is for a taxi driver to pick you up and then drive you to a secluded area where his colleagues jump into the back seat with you -- usually one on each side -- and rob you. This can escalate to an express kidnapping as well if they choose to abduct you and drive you to an ATM machine to withdraw money. In more serious cases there is the risk of serious assault, rape or murder.

Therefore hailing street taxis should be avoided and in many locations caution should be used when using any taxis.

Never get in a taxi that already has any other passengers in it. In some countries taxi drivers will try to pick up multiple fares. If this customary in your location tell the driver you want a "private taxi" and if necessary pay extra.

Sit directly behind the driver. This might seem weird or awkward but it's very difficult for the driver to control you when you are in this position and it's easier for you to control him should the situation require you to.

Lock doors and roll up the windows. This should be pretty standard practice when traveling in a vehicle in the developing world anyway

-- even more so when in a taxi.

Be alert to pedestrians on either side of the vehicle when stopped - either in traffic, at a red light, etc. Be prepared to exit the vehicle quickly if someone should try to get in. Also watch for signs of any communication or signaling between the driver and pedestrians or people in other vehicles.

Don't accept food, drink or chewing gum if offered by the driver. In some crimes involving taxis the passenger has been drugged as a precursor to a robbery or sexual assault.

Self-Driving vs. Hiring a Driver -- the Pros and Cons

One of the questions for expatriates and many travelers is whether to hire a local driver or drive themselves. There are pros and cons associated with both choices and its important to recognize and consider them when making a decision.

This discussion focuses on expatriates and travelers in developing countries where this decision is much more critical and the potential pitfalls of making the wrong choice are much greater. Let's look at each option:

Hiring a Driver:

Pros:

The local driver will/should know the geography of the area, can find different locations more readily than you might be able to and will know local traffic patterns at different hours of the day, etc.

The local driver will know the driving etiquette in the area and will be less likely to inadvertently cause offense to other drivers, etc.

The local driver will know the proper procedure when stopped by the police and will know how to deal with the situation.

With a hired driver you are free to focus on situational awareness and detecting possible surveillance or threats in the environment without the distraction of driving in an unfamiliar city, following directions, etc.

If you are involved in an accident the driver will generally be the one held responsible and not you.

You can assign the driver to guard the car when you are at meetings, etc. Therefore the car is not left unattended and is not as vulnerable to being tampered with, having items stolen from it or having the vehicle itself stolen.

You don't need to worry about parking the vehicle when you disembark to do other things such as attend meetings, go shopping, etc. The driver can remain with the vehicle and pick you up when requested.

Cons:

You are literally trusting your life to the driver. A bad or reckless driver can be very dangerous and the driver may not be trained to deal effectively with a security incident should one occur.

You give up some independence relying on the driver. The driver may be tardy, get lost or otherwise compromise your effectiveness.

You will have some level of OPSEC risk with the driver. The driver will know where you go, who you meet with and other information that may make you vulnerable.

Self-Driving:

Pros:

You take your fate in your own hands literally. You are much more in control of your own life when you self-drive.

You can potentially respond better to a security incident. If you already have - or if you obtain quality training in security/evasive driving techniques you will be better prepared than almost all but the best trained drivers to respond to a security incident when you are traveling in a vehicle.

You have greater personal and operational security because you do not need to advise another person of your plans.

You will become familiar with the area where you are living much more quickly because by self-driving you will be forced to learn the local streets, etc.

Cons:

You are liable in the event you are involved in a vehicle accident. As a foreigner you may be judged to be at fault even if you are not. This can result in you being jailed even for minor infractions. This is one of the greatest vulnerabilities of self-driving in developing world countries.

Traffic patterns and driving styles are usually very different (and in many ways much worse) than most western visitors and expatriates are accustomed to in their home countries.

You are potentially more vulnerable if stopped by local law enforcement or security forces while driving. They may see this as an opportunity to extort money from you.

Parking can be difficult in many congested third world cities and finding safe, acceptable parking near your destination can be very time consuming and difficult.

If you need to leave the vehicle unattended in some locations depending on the security situation you may need to do a search of the vehicle before entering it and departing. Not only is this time consuming but it can leave you vulnerable while you are distracted and focused on searching the vehicle.

In conclusion the decision on whether to self-drive or hire a driver is a personal one that should be made based on the environment you are operating in, your capabilities, the resources available to you and a review of the considerations above.

Considerations for Self-Driving

When possible it may be best to avoid self-driving overseas, especially in developing world countries. For one thing you are very exposed if you get into an accident -- there is a risk both from local authorities and also from any crowd that may gather. Generally in the developing world driving practices are much more erratic than what most of us are accustomed to. That combined with an oopsy-daisy attitude to life and death and fundamental safety matters in many places make traveling by vehicle in particular and self-driving in particular a significant vulnerability.

In some cases however it may be unavoidable or impractical especially for expatriates or those on long term temporary assignments who must maintain a level of mobility and independence. Even in these cases if you are located outside of Europe or some of the more developed Asian or Latin American countries it's probably best to employ a reliable local driver. If you can't or won't you should at least review the following considerations (these can also be useful teaching points to train a local driver as well):

Consider getting some formal driving training in both accident avoidance and evasive driving. You may need to do this prior to deployment as options for this type of training may be limited or nonexistent where you are going.

Conduct a map reconnaissance and a route analysis prior to driving in a unfamiliar area.

Bring an international drivers permit even if its not required in the country where you are driving. This may be helpful if stopped by local authorities.

Always ensure that your vehicle is in good working condition. This seems like common sense but situations that can be annoying in your home country can be life threatening in more high-risk locations.

Make sure you maintain your fuel tank at half or higher. This is especially true in areas where fuel may be scarce or where fuel stations may have very long queues.

Know your recommended tire pressure and check it regularly.

Make sure you have a serviceable spare tire in your vehicle along with the appropriate tools and know how to change it.

Always strive to allow maneuver room between your vehicle and the vehicle in front of you when stopped in traffic. You should be able to see the bottom of the tires of the car in front of you.

When parking you should back into the space whenever possible. This will allow you a better field of vision and the ability to depart more rapidly.

In high threat environments you should avoid leaving your vehicle parked unattended in a public location. If it must be left unattended the vehicle should be searched prior to entering it and departing.

When traveling in heavy traffic you should be especially aware of what is going on around you both for purposes of accident avoidance and also because of the vulnerability to criminals who prey on motorists stuck in traffic.

Consider practicing driving in reverse. In many instances fancy evasive maneuvers may not be applicable even if you know how to employ them. Sometimes if you detect a problem up ahead the best solution is to reverse until you can safely turn the car and get out of the area.

☐

If you get involved in an accident in may be prudent to leave the area and go to a safe haven like a police station (in some locations this may not be that safe of a haven) to report the incident. Most of us are conditioned as drivers not to leave the scene of an accident but it may not be safe to remain in some locations. A crowd will likely form and you as the foreigner will likely be seen as being at fault whether you were or not. Vigilante "justice" and lynchings are common in many parts of the world and local authorities may be powerless to intervene or may willfully turn a blind eye.

Use caution when approaching roadblocks and make an assessment as soon as possible. This is a topic that will be discussed in greater depth separately but suffice to say if you are living or traveling somewhere were roadblocks erected by police, military, paramilitary groups or others you should become familiar with the procedures and routine for safe passage and recognize that approaching and passing through a roadblock can be a potentially dangerous situation.

Vehicular travel in the developing world presents some risks - both related to safety and security - especially if you are driving yourself.

Working with Local Drivers

If you are a traveler or an expatriate who chooses to use a local driver instead of self-driving (see our separate discussion on deciding whether to self-drive or use a driver and the pros and cons of each) then we'll look at working with local drivers.

When ever possible get a vetted local driver. Sources for drivers can include security companies, transportation companies and hotels. When possible its best to have a driver who has had formal security driver training although this is relatively rare in most countries in the developing world and should not be expected.

You should look for a driver with some type of general driver training for proficiency and safety purposes. The bar is very low in many countries to obtain a driver's license. In almost all locations your greatest risk will be getting into a vehicle accident and not being the victim of an attack so having a driver who understands and employs the fundamentals of safe driving will be a huge asset. If you are an expatriate or long term visitor it may be worthwhile to invest in the driver by getting him some training.

Get a driver who speaks at least decent English unless you are proficient in the local language. This will help avert much confusion, missed pick-ups, etc. that can be caused by the language barrier.

If a long-term visitor or expatriate get to know as much about your driver as possible -- where he lives, his family, his ethnic or tribal affiliation (where applicable). You will be much less likely to have trouble with a driver who knows he is potentially vulnerable to repercussions.

When working with local drivers here are some general guidelines to follow in most situations and in most locations:

Make expectations clear to the driver at the beginning. Much of working or living in the developing world is about managing expectations: yours and the driver's.

Use reverse planning and pad in extra time. Concepts of time and punctuality are often not the same in much of the world. Additionally in some cities traffic is so congested it is prudent to have the driver arrive early to ensure he is there when you need him.

Don't give the driver too much information in advance about your itinerary. Let him know where you need to go and when at the time and not in advance. There is no benefit and significant vulnerability to you. Even if you trust your driver and have worked with him for a while you don't know what external pressures he might be under. If someone is threatening his family to force him to provide information to target you then he'll give you up. By limiting his advanced knowledge of your movements you reduce this risk.

Treat your driver with respect and take care of his welfare. Be courteous to your driver and give him opportunities for breaks, enough rest between assignments, etc. If you go out to eat at a restaurant consider sending a meal out to the driver if he is waiting in the vehicle outside. I know of anecdotal cases in Latin America and the Philippines where people were set up for burglary, robbery and kidnapping by their drivers and other domestic employees. There is no excuse for treating your driver badly and it arguably increases your vulnerability to do so.

Remember the driver is not your friend. As a follow up to the point above - take care of the driver and be courteous to him but don't be too familiar. Westerners - and Americans in particular tend to be very egalitarian which may not be the best approach. Avoid taking meals with and/or socializing with the driver. In most traditional societies roles are very clearly defined. Being too familiar with the driver may confuse him and undermine the working relationship that you have with him. It may also result in a deterioration in his performance.

- Keep any gratuities reasonable and in keeping with local custom. Its fine to reward a driver with a tip for good performance but in a poor country giving a driver a $50 or $100 tip for a few days work can be the equivalent of tipping him his monthly salary. This can at a minimum (1) cause the driver to get confused and expect this level of tip from everyone (2) confirm how "rich" you are. It may also cause problems with the driver's employer (if hired through a third party) if you are giving him the equivalent of a month's salary for a tip.

When working with local drivers its important to keep these principles in mind -- generally speaking they will make the relationship more productive and effective for both of you.

Route Analysis and Selection

Whether you are self-driving or using a driver route analysis and route selection are key elements of your security when moving

59

around your overseas location. Route selection is important because:

It allows you to avoid known danger areas such as high-crime neighborhoods or to implement countermeasures if the area is unavoidable.

Provides you with alternate routes to avoid time and place predictability.

Helps you identify choke points and other potential attack sites so that you can raise your awareness level in these areas.

Helps you identify zones of predictability that you must pass through regardless of the route you use. Your origin point and destination are two zones of predictability but there may be others.

Allows you to identify safe havens along the route that can be utilized if needed.

The first stage of a route analysis is a thorough map reconnaissance to determine potential routes between the point of origin and destination. Whenever possible its best to use two or more maps of the same area to compare features to get the most accurate picture. Large scale maps with lots of detail are best if available. Online mapping and satellite imagery tools like Google Earth are also great to incorporate.

Once you have plotted the potential routes on the map you should drive them -- ideally several times at the different hours of the day that you will be traveling. This will let you verify the observations that you made on your map recon and also will let you see traffic flow at various points on the routes. You can also verify the location and accessibility of safe havens you have identified, etc. During this phase you may also want to time the different routes at different hours of the day.

The degree of detail you go into on route analysis will vary depending on a number of factors:

Duration of time you are spending at the location may dictate the level of depth. If you are there for weeks or months it may make more sense to do a detailed study versus only staying for a few days.

Likelihood of being specifically targeted. Obviously if you know or think there is a real risk you may be specifically targeted then you need to concentrate on route variance and will likely want to invest the time to do a detailed route analysis.

General security environment. Even if you are not especially concerned about being specifically targeted it is still reasonable you will want to do a more detailed route analysis in a higher threat environment.

Route Selection Considerations:

Generally major roads with free flowing traffic are preferable to smaller side streets where may be easier for assailants to ambush you. This may not always be true depending on local traffic patterns.

Routes should avoid or at least minimize the need to drive through identified danger areas like high crime neighborhoods and other known threat locations.

Choose routes that avoid choke points to the degree possible.

Zones of predictability and choke points should at least provide good observation when possible.

Routes will multiple safe havens located on them are preferable.

Vehicle Security Self-Search

If you are working or living in an area where there is a significant terrorist threat or if you are someone who is in an at-risk category or may be specifically targeted you should consider conducting a vehicle search for possible improvised explosive devices (IEDs) anytime your vehicle is parked where it is accessible and is unattended.

I do not suggest that most people need to incorporate this technique into their personal security program. It's a very specific response to a particular type of threat but those who are operating in high-risk areas where booby-trapping of vehicles occurs and those who may be targeted for assassination should utilize this technique.

There is a lot of material available on this subject and it is taught in many executive protection and security driving courses. If you are looking for a more detailed discussion of vehicle search techniques a very good resource is "Survival Driving: Staying Alive on the World's Most Dangerous Roads" by Robert Deatherage.

I will give a much briefer version here that nonetheless provides a good starting point.

You should begin the search with a walk-around and a check of all external areas of the vehicle. A flashlight will be useful for this. The wheel wells, undercarriage of the vehicle, bumpers, etc. should be checked. Additionally you should look for any signs of forced entry or tampering with the vehicle.

The hood and engine compartment should be checked next. You may want to weigh the hood down with something as you open it to control the speed with which it rises. Check for any wires, fishing line, etc. running from the hood to the engine compartment. Once open check around the engine. Be familiar with the engine compartment so you can better notice something out of place.

After checking the engine compartment move on to the trunk. As with the hood weigh it down to control the speed as it opens and check for tripwires connected to the trunk lid. Check the interior to include the tool compartment, etc.

Once the trunk has been checked begin the interior search by first looking through the windows for anything out of place. As a general rule its best to reduce clutter in the vehicle to facilitate detecting any potential threat.

Enter the vehicle cautiously - preferably using the least used door (such as one of the rear passenger doors). Check for tripwires when opening the door as you did with the hood and trunk. Once inside check all compartments, underseats and under mats.

Suffice to say if you find a suspicious item don't attempt to detach or disarm it yourself - even if it appears to be a simple device there may be hidden anti-handling measures. Call the local authorities or your security point of contact to arrange for an explosive ordnance disposal team response.

Remember however that if there is an explosive device in the vehicle -- it was more than likely placed in an easily accessible place.

Hotel Security

Many travelers view their hotel in a foreign city as a safe sanctuary where nothing can happen. While hotels – particularly good hotels that have been carefully selected – can be a good safe haven in many respects they can also be a focal point for criminal activity and other hazards so it's very important not to drop your guard.

When checking in ensure that the reception desk doesn't announce your room number to everyone in the lobby. Well-trained staff at good hotels won't do this — they will write the number down, usually on the paper sleeve that holds your room key. If they do announce your room number then request another room and ask that they write the number down.

While at the reception desk maintain contact with your luggage whenever possible. Ideally you should be in physical contact with your foot or leg so that if someone tries to move it or take it you will be immediately aware.

Don't be afraid to ask a member of the hotel staff to escort you to your room if this makes you feel more comfortable.

On the way to your room observe the location of the nearest fire exit and count the number of doors between your room and the fire exit. If there is a fire and you need to evacuate the hotel you may be crawling down a smoke-filled hallway and unable to see the exit sign. You should know in which direction and how many doors you need to go to find an exit. This only takes a minute to do and with practice becomes second nature.

After getting settled in the room you may want to go back and confirm this as well as find a secondary exit and even consider going into the fire stairwell and walking downstairs to be familiar with it. Be cautious of opening any exit doors though as they may be alarmed. Also be cautious that you do not get locked in the stairwell. In some buildings only certain floors are re-entry floors and in some extreme cases there is no re-entry from the fire stairs to any floor except the street level.

When you get to the room immediately check it to be sure nobody is concealed inside. This means the closets and wardrobe, inside the bathroom (to include the shower if there is a curtain or door), etc.

Keep the door locked when you are in the room to include using the chain or sliding bar. Seriously consider using door stops.
.
Use the "Do Not Disturb" sign liberally to include whenever you are in the room and most times when you go out. Do not use the "Make up my Room" sign for maid service. Instead call housekeeping and request service when needed.

Consider leaving the TV or radio on when you are out of the room if this is possible. In some hotels the room key needs to be inserted into an outlet on the wall to provide power so this may be difficult to do. It is however an option to bring an old card key from a previous stay at another hotel and use that to insert in the outlet when you leave the room.

When exiting the elevator to your floor check the hallway in both directions before walking to your room. In some hotels the hallway may have alcoves or offsets where people can conceal themselves without being seen. Be especially vigilant when walking down hallways of this type. Likewise check the hallway in both directions when you exit your room.

Have your room key ready in your hand so you are not fumbling at your door when you get there.

If you see anyone loitering in the hall or behaving in a suspicious or abnormal manner do not go to your room but instead return to the lobby or another safe location.

Do not open your room to anyone claiming to be staff that you are not expecting. Call the reception desk to verify their identity.

When you are out of your room consider using a very small piece of paper inserted between the jam and the door as a "tell" to indicate if anyone has entered your room. This must be small enough to be unnoticed by others and artfully placed to remain undetected.

Keep a small flashlight by your bedside so you will always have access to a light source in the event of a power outage and so it is accessible if you need to use it to evacuate the hotel in the middle of the night.

Leave your clothes with valuable items such as your passport, wallet etc. in the pockets and your shoes nearby so that you can put them on rapidly should you need to get up and evacuate quickly.

Avoid using the room safe for valuables. These safes are easily compromised, especially by staff and will be the first place someone looks if they come into your room.

Hotel Selection

Selecting a hotel is one of the most important considerations when traveling. The hotel is your home away from home and maybe some travelers incorrectly also view it as a sanctuary from the dangers that are present at the location.

There are several key factors to look at when selecting a hotel. There are two schools of thought on choosing a hotel: using a name-brand property vs. using a low profile hotel. Which hotel to choose depends largely on the type of threat at the location in question.

In locations where the primary threat is opportunistic, economically-motivated crime there are good arguments for choosing a large, western-brand hotel which is likely to have better security measures, a quality control and audit process administered by a regional office and these types of hotels are more likely to keep out undesirable people.

For cities where the primary concern is terrorism it may be advisable to choose a lower profile hotel that is not as likely to be targeted by terrorists.

This is not a hard and fast rule by any means and really requires a detailed examination of the hotel options and different threats at your destination.

When possible it is best to try to choose a room between the 2nd and 7th floor. The 2nd floor or higher makes it generally more difficult for a burglar to access from the street. Most fire service equipment - especially in the developing world can't reach higher than the 7th floor. In locations where terrorism is a concern it is best to request a room on the backside of the hotel rather than the street side. This provides some additional protection against a vehicle-borne improvised explosive device (VBIED) being detonated in front of the hotel.

There is some debate about whether or not to get a room near the fire exit or not. In the event of a fire in the hotel you want to navigate as short a distance as possible from your room to the fire exit through a smoke-filled hallway. On the other side -- there is a credible concern about having a room near the fire exit as criminals can potentially lurk in the fire stairwell and victimize people as they enter or leave their rooms.

Whenever possible its best to avoid rooms that adjoin other rooms.

Of course all of these preference items such as floor, room location, etc. are subject to availability in the real world. Often you won't be able to make these choices but it is still good to understand the different considerations.

Threat-Based Hotel Selection Criteria

When using security criteria in selecting hotels its important to consider the prevalent threats at the location in question. In general there are going to be one or both of two main categories of threat to consider: General Crime and Terrorism.

While there may be some overlap -- an some countermeasures such as access control and employee vetting may be useful for counteracting both -- there are some selection criteria that may differ greatly. Sometimes - though rarely they may contradict each other.

Criteria to look for when the hotel is located in an area where general crime is the main risk:

Good access control. While hotel properties are typically open to the public the presence of hotel staff at the entrances who are alert and greeting people entering the property is a positive sign. Ideally these employees have received some training and are looking for personnel who don't belong or seem out of place. Likewise service entrances and other non-public entry points should be guarded or closed and locked.

Presence and prevalence of CCTV cameras. While cameras have a limited ability to stop crimes from happening and are more useful as an investigative tool after an incident occurs they are of some use as a deterrent - especially for lower level petty criminals. A quality CCTV system can indicate that the management is invested in security and focused on it.

Visible security personnel in the lobby and patrolling public areas. In some African hotels guards are also posted on each floor.

Card access control on the elevator. While this can be defeated by people piggy-backing on the elevator its still a good measure.

Card key use on guest doors as opposed to traditional metal keys.

Security bolts and chains on room doors.

Limited or no re-entry floors on fire stairs. Fire stairwells provide criminals a method of moving from floor-to-floor discreetly. If it is impossible to re-enter floors once in the staircase and the only exit is a ground level fire exit door it restricts this avenue for criminals.

Employee vetting process. Hotel employees have considerable access to guest rooms and property as part of their official duties. Normally the only way to determine employee vetting is through an formal assessment of the hotel and meetings with hotel management or by speaking to someone that has conducted such an assessment.

Employee security training and training of guard staff. Again - a formal assessment will usually be necessary to obtain this information.

In locations where the principal or greatest threat is terrorism there are some different criteria. Arguably the two greatest terrorist threats to a hotel are a vehicle borne improvised explosive device (VBIED) and a Mumbai-style attack on the hotel with small arms and grenades. There is also a risk of suicide bombers entering the hotel or even registering as guests or obtaining employment at the hotel as occurred in the Jakarta attacks. Here are some primary considerations:

Setback / standoff from the road. This is one of the main considerations in mitigating vehicle bomb attacks. Unfortunately in many urban areas around the world this can be difficult to achieve.

Vehicle access control. Vehicle checkpoints where incoming vehicles are searched prior to being permitted access are of key importance. Chicane approaches are also sometimes used to prevent a vehicle from gaining speed to ram into the hotel lobby.

No underground parking or heavily restricted underground parking.

No parking close to the hotel building or very restricted parking.

Protective shatterproof film on windows.

Lower level building or guest rooms located to rear of hotel.

Presence of armed security personnel or police/military forces on site.

Not located next to / or in very close proximity to other high value targets like government buildings.

Good evacuation and emergency plans that are regularly exercised. You would need to meet with hotel management to determine this.

A surveillance detection program. While relatively rare one major US chain does this at select properties.

There are some rare occasions when criteria that may be good for one kind of threat may not be good for another. One example is that a low-rise hotel with separate units or connected bungalows might be good where the local threat is terrorism as the property is likely to be less attractive for a vehicle bomb attack. However this type of configuration where rooms have their own entrance to the outside presents additional risks in a criminal threat environment.

When selecting a hotel the threat environment is an important consideration.

Using Rubber Doorstops to Enhance your Security in Hotels

Inexpensive rubber door stops are a great tool for adding an additional layer of security when traveling. While many hotel rooms have a chain or sliding bar that can and should be engaged when in the room, these measures can be easily defeated if someone tries to force the door. More alarming some hotels do not have these features at all leaving the guest to rely on the room lock alone. In most hotels the majority of staff have access to a pass key giving them unrestricted access to all the rooms.

When traveling you can throw the doorstop in your bag. It ways next to nothing and takes up almost no room. You might even consider taking two doorstops in your bag in case you get a room that also has a door to an adjoining room -- then you can block both doors. Generally its advisable to request a room that doesn't connect to an adjoining room but the realities of travel sometimes mean you may find yourself in that situation.

There are commercial security doorstops on the market that incorporate an audible alarm into the doorstop. These are relatively inexpensive and can be a good option. One thing to note though is that because they incorporate batteries and wiring circuits they may draw attention if detected on x-ray machines at airports or other venues. Because they are an unusual shape and incorporate those components there is the possibility that you will need to remove them from your bag and explain what they are to security screeners in a foreign country who might be accustomed to seeing mobile phones or computers but not security doorstops.

This is not a major issue but something to consider, especially if you want to avoid scrutiny in foreign airports. The regular rubber doorstops will cause the intruder to either break-off their effort to enter your room or smash the door down which should be alarm enough itself to wake the heaviest sleeper.

Residential Security

Expatriates and long term visitors who will be using private accommodation rather than a hotel need to look at security considerations when selecting a residence.

The first consideration should be the location and neighborhood. You clearly want to identify a safe or safer neighborhood for obvious reasons. Unfortunately in many places crime statistics are not maintained by the police or are not accurate if they are kept so you will likely need to interview expatriates, local residents and diplomatic missions, etc. for anecdotal input. You may also want to consider areas where other expatriates reside and make contacts for mutual assistance. The downside of these expatriate-heavy areas is that they may be considered a target-rich environment for both criminals and extremist groups. This concern has to be weighed against the positive aspects of having other expatriates nearby.

You will also want to look at proximity to police and fire stations, hospitals and supermarkets, grocery stores, etc. Depending on the security environment you may also want to consider avoiding locations near high profile targets that may be selected for attack by terrorists or may be a focal point in the event of a coup attempt, etc. Some examples are government buildings, diplomatic missions, presidential palace, military barracks and so forth.

Physical location: In addition to selecting a safe neighborhood you want to assess the physical layout and street conditions. You want to identify residential areas with light pedestrian and vehicle traffic. Congested areas with high levels of vehicles and pedestrians provide surveillants and potential attackers with cover to operate. Ideally you want a neighborhood where strangers or loiterers stand out and are readily identified.

You also want to avoid cul de sacs, one-way streets, dead-end streets and other features that limit or restrict your options for movement.

Given the fact that the entry point of a residence is a favorite attack site both for economically-motivated crime like carjacking and also targeted kidnappings and killings you want to ensure that you have several options for movement.

Apartment vs. Single Family Dwelling: the next thing to consider is whether to choose an apartment or single family house. Generally speaking in most cases an apartment offers better security, especially if it is in a building with a good level of security. We discuss some considerations of each.

First let's briefly discuss layered security or defense in depth: Whether you choose a house or an apartment you want to pick a location that offers multiple layers of security that an intruder needs to overcome. This will (1) deter many criminals that are looking for an easy target (2) buy time for a response team to arrive (3) potentially buy you time to seek shelter, call for help, etc.

Apartment: When choosing an apartment you should look for the following criteria:

A guard, doorman or concierge who physically inspects visitors and controls access.

A vehicle checkpoint if applicable.

As with hotel rooms you want to select an apartment between the 2nd and 7th floors so it is high enough to deter burglars but low enough to be reached by fire-fighting equipment.

Multiple entrances and exits that are guarded or where access is effectively controlled.

CCTV system and other physical security measures.

House: If choosing a house you will want to consider the following factors:

Walled property. This is common in most single family dwellings in the developing world. The wall should be high enough to deter an intruder from scaling it.

Wall security enhancements: the wall should be reinforced by being topped with barbed wire/razor wire, broken glass, etc. In many places in Africa electrified fences are used on top of residential walls as well.

Guards: employing a guard or guards to be posted at the entrance both deters potential criminals, provides a human response at the first layer and if properly trained a set of eyes and ears on the perimeter.

CCTV: This can be useful as a deterrent, a means of remotely investigating a possible intrusion and an investigative tool. Ideally where it is legal you should position some cameras to observe the street and public areas outside your residence.

Alarm System: An alarm system can be a great asset in providing an early warning to you. It should be linked to a central monitoring station. Many systems also have a duress button that can be manually triggered and some also have portable duress button that can be carried on your person within the home.

Alarm Response Capability: In most developing world countries police response to crimes in progress is unreliable. Therefore there is usually a plethora of private sector security responders who provide alarm response. This is definitely worth considering and is a great asset for your personal security. You do need to invest the effort and energy in vetting and selecting a good provider.

Safe Room: In locations where home invasion robberies and other violent intrusions are a concern or if you are at at-risk or targeted person then you should look at building a safe room within your home and stocking it with essential items to sustain yourself.

You'll also want to consider quality locks, reinforced doors, window guards, shatterproof window film and other physical measures.

Confrontational Crime

Common Carjacking Methods

Carjacking remains a serious threat in many developing countries. For our purposes in this discussion we will broaden the definition of carjacking and consider not only forcible theft of the vehicle but also armed robbery of the vehicle's occupants and/or kidnapping. The motivation of the criminals is generally less important than the tactics and methods used.

Blocking vehicle -- this is a classic method used in robberies, kidnappings and assassinations worldwide. When you are driving slowly or are stopped at a predetermined location - usually a chokepoint - a vehicle will pull in front of you preventing your movement or in some cases two vehicles, one to the front and one to the rear will block you in. While you are unable to escape the perpetrators will either deploy from the vehicle or from hiding places along the road and carry out the crime - whether it is robbery, kidnapping or assassination. In Nairobi, Kenya there has been a trend of blocking the vehicle from the rear. Most homes there are surrounded by a wall with an entrance gate for vehicles. When a driver arrives at their home and waits for their guard or other domestic employee to open the gate for them a blocking vehicle pulls up behind them pinning the victims car between the gate and the blocking vehicle. The perpetrators then deploy from their vehicle and carry-out the crime.

The Bump - the carjackers will bump your vehicle from behind and cause a minor accident. When you stop to check the damage they will victimize you.

Car Trouble - Another vehicle will pull alongside or a pedestrian will come over and indicate you have a flat tire or some other car problem to get you to pull over and get out of the vehicle.

Good Samaritan - The criminals will simulate a car accident, pose as distressed motorists or injured victims to entice you to stop and give aid.

Overtaking Vehicle Attack - there is no ruse involved here. This is an overt attack where the assailants will drive up from the rear and force your vehicle to pull over - either by: (1) using their vehicle as a weapon for force you off the road, (2) displaying weapons (3) or in some cases firing on your vehicle.

Halted Traffic Attack - another common overt attack. This is similar to the Blocking Vehicle Attack except natural traffic conditions provide the "blocking vehicles". In this case the criminals know the local traffic patterns and select a location where at a specific time of day traffic creates a chokepoint. The attackers then assault the vehicle while its stuck in traffic. They will typically attack on foot or frequently on motorcycles. This is more common when the intent is to rob the vehicle's occupants as its difficult (but possible) to conduct a kidnapping this way and more difficult to steal the vehicle due to limited egress options.

Kidnapping

Kidnapping Primer

One critical element when discussing personal security, especially in the developing world is to have an understanding of the various types of kidnapping that exist and the associated mitigation and prevention strategies that you can employ.

First off, it's important to note that in the US in particular and most of Western Europe kidnapping for economic or political reasons is a relatively rare crime. One exception is "Tiger Kidnapping" which is prevalent in parts of Europe.

Furthermore an overwhelming number of kidnapping incidents are resolved and usually quickly. This is not true in developing countries so those who work or travel there need to be aware of the associated risks and the methodologies used.
First off let's discuss the primary types of kidnappings in the US and then move on to the variations prevalent elsewhere in the world.

Parental/Custody Kidnapping: These incidents, which make up the majority of the kidnappings in the US arise from custody disputes where a parent or other relative abducts a child or children.

Predatory Kidnapping: An abduction where the victim is taken by a predator to commit a sexual or other violent crime where there is no economic motivation. These incidents are the reason why many crime prevention experts in the US warn about the risk of being taken to "crime scene 2".

Other types of kidnapping which are more prevalent in developing nations:

Kidnap for Ransom: a traditional kidnapping where the victim is abducted and held while the victim's family or employer is contacted and a ransom is demanded.

Express Kidnapping: Sometimes also called a lightning kidnapping. This is an increasingly prevalent crime where the victim is selected quickly and held for a short period of time usually from several hours to a day or two. Sometimes several days. The victim is typically taken to ATM machines and made to withdraw the daily maximum. In some cases the victim's family may also be required to pay a small ransom.

Political Kidnapping: Kidnapping a victim or victims with the intent to exchange them for prisoners being held by the authorities or for some political concession from the government.

Virtual Kidnapping: Not really a kidnapping at all but more an extortion. The "kidnappers" identify when a potential victim is incommunicado for a particular period of time usually due to travel, being in a movie or similar event. They then contact the victim's family and claim to be holding the victim and demand a small ransom to be paid immediately. The family typically panics and unable to reach the victim, pays the ransom.

Tiger Kidnapping: This is a bit of an exception to my comments above as this crime is somewhat prevalent in the Republic of Ireland and the UK. Typically the victim is a bank manager or other financial services manager with access to cash or other valuables. In these cases the victim's residence is invaded and the family held hostage. While the family is being held by part of the kidnap gang the bank manager is taken to his place of business and forced to turn over cash or other valuables to secure the release of his family.

There are also some rarer types of kidnapping that most expatriates and travelers are unlikely to encounter:

Revenge kidnappings: these most often occur to persons involved in some type of criminal activity -- often done by one criminal group against members of another in order to send a message. These incidents also occur occasionally in areas where there are family, tribal or clan rivalries but again are usually restricted to members of the rival clan.

Bridal kidnappings: In some parts of Central Asia this is still used as a mating ritual of sorts. A man kidnaps a woman as his prospective bride and holds her for several days. At this point her honor is called into question and her family agrees to her marrying the kidnapper.

This is by no means an exhaustive list but most other types of kidnap events could likely be classified as a subset of the above types or refers to a tactic for kidnapping such as miracle fishing kidnaps or mass kidnaps.

Express Kidnapping

Express kidnapping - also sometimes called lightening kidnapping - is a prevalent crime in much of the developing world. While is particularly common in Latin America it occurs globally - I am personally aware of incidents in locations as diverse as Kazakhstan and China.

Tourists and business travelers are much more likely to be victims of an express kidnapping than a more traditional kidnap for ransom. The typical method of operation is to grab the victim and take him or her to different ATMs to with draw money until the daily limit is met. In some case the victim will be held for a day or two to withdraw the limit for each day. On occasion the victim will also be held until a relatively small ransom is delivered by the victim's family or company -- turning it into a mini kidnap for ransom.

Victims are still selected but the selection process is much more rapid than in a traditional kidnap. On occasion the victim may be grabbed off the street and at other times the event may start as a carjacking (this is common in Nairobi, Kenya for example) or a taxi driver may be involved.

Perpetrators of an express kidnap are looking to turn a quick buck and dump the victim. They usually do not have the infrastructure or desire the hold the victim for more than a few days. They are also usually less professional than traditional kidnappers although in recent years some express kidnappers have shown increasing sophistication. One express kidnapping ring in Caracas, Venezuela was gathering personal data on their victims to (a) assign some level of value to the person and (b) for intimidation purposes as the kidnappers can locate the victim, their family members or associates in the future if the victim should go to the police.

Some ways to avoid or mitigate an express kidnapping:

As always situational awareness is paramount. There will be a victim selection process so be aware of people who may be taking unusual interest in you and move to safety as quickly as possible.

Avoid using ATMs on the street where you may be targeted. Try to use ATMs located within a hotel, bank or shopping mall and be especially vigilant at these times.

Be very careful when using taxis as taxi crime and express kidnappings are often closely linked.

Be alert to carjacking techniques and develop and employ countermeasures. As with taxi crimes, in some locations carjackings frequently escalate into express kidnapping.

Be cautious about drugs such as scopolamine, ativan or rohypnol being used to incapacitate you to facilitate an express kidnapping. This is also a common modus operandi in certain locations around the world.

Consider carrying an ATM card linked to an account with limit funds so the account can be emptied quickly, hopefully limiting the length of your detention.

Devil's Breath and the Ativan Gang

An alarming trend that has been occurring in different places around the world is the use of drugs in facilitating crimes like robbery, sexual assault and kidnapping. These incidents have occurred in locations as varied as Colombia, the Philippines and India.

While most Americans may be aware of the use of drugs such as Rohypnol and GHB to facilitate date rape, many do not know how common these drugging incidents are overseas.

In May 2012 a tour guide in New Delhi was arrested for drugging and robbing lone tourists. He met most of them in the area of the Chandi Chowk and Red Fort, offered them food laced with an unknown drug that incapacitated them and then robbed them and dumped them in remote areas. While this particular modus operandi has not been that common in India it is very common in other areas.

Colombia is one of the best known locations for this type of activity. Scopolamine - known locally as Burandanga - is used to facilitate crime by rendering the victim into a compliant, zombie-like state. When the victim recovers he or she will usually have limited or no memory of the incident. A recent documentary called the "The Devil's Breath" brought the dangers of Scopolamine to a broad audience but this drug has been used for nefarious purposes in Colombia and neighboring countries for quite a while. Methods of deployment can include everything from spiking food or drink to blowing it in the victim's face.

In the Philippines the "Ativan Gang" (probably actually numerous groups using the same or similar methods) has preyed on victims by drugging them with Ativan and robbing them. In some cases an attractive female will strike up a conversation with a lone male, go out for cocktails and spike his drink. Then she and her accomplices will rob him. In another variation a group of matronly older women will initiate a relationship with a tourist and invite him or her for a meal. They will subsequently spike the food and/or drink and rob the tourist. There are other methods as well but these are two of the most prevalent.

Sometimes with these stories it can be difficult to separate truth from urban myth but there are enough verifiable incidents to establish that this is a concern -- in particular in some of the locations mentioned. The scary thing about this type of crime is that it can render even the strongest, most competent fighter helpless. The only remedy is to be aware of this threat and practice avoidance. Be wary of unsolicited approaches by strangers. Some of these can be very convincing. Don't accept food, drink or chewing gum from anyone you don't know well. If you are at a bar or similar establishment don't leave your drink unattended and monitor it carefully. Also -- going out in pairs or groups may also help guard against this type of threat.

The Miracle Fishing Kidnap Threat

We have repeatedly discussed the pre-operational steps that occur prior to most crimes from similar robbery to assassination and perhaps most notably kidnapping. These steps include things like surveillance and target selection. There is at least one type of crime where this does not occur however -- at least not in the typical sense -- mass kidnappings or "miracle fishing". Mass kidnappings often called miracle fishing or pesca milagrosa have been perhaps most common in Latin America, in particular Colombia although it does occur other places as well.

Classic pesca milagrosa reached its zenith in Colombia in the 1990s and early 2000s and was largely perpetrated by the two main leftist guerilla groups, the ELN and the FARC and to a degree by right-wing paramilitary groups. Most mass kidnappings have involved victims being abducted at an improvised roadblock although in some cases kidnappers enter an establishment like a restaurant or hotel and take all the patrons hostage.

Mass kidnapping may be less common than other types of kidnaps and it may be more geographically isolated to some areas like rural Colombia --- so why spend time talking about it? One key reasons is that most typical proactive security measures have limit usefulness compared to other types of situations.

While there may be a number of ways it can occur (piracy and hostage taking in the horn of Africa or a mass kidnapping from a tourist park as occurred in Uganda) the classic example usually involves a roadblock or unlawful checkpoint -- especially in the classic "miracle fishing" scenario in Colombia. The term "Miracle Fishing" refers to the way the perpetrators figuratively "cast a net" and gather "fish". They keep the big fish and throw back the little ones.

In these situations the kidnappers will typically set up a roadblock on a stretch of road - sometimes over the crest of a hill or at a blind curve in a road to avoid giving the victim advanced warning. As cars pull up the roadblock the drivers and passengers are pulled from the vehicle and either assessed at the scene or more likely detained, moved from the scene to a secure location and assessed for valuation at that point. During the assessment phase the kidnappers will try to determine the value if each victim and then keeping the high-value victims and releasing the low-value victims. In some cases the valuation phase can be quite sophisticated to include using laptop computers and access to bank information. One of the most noteworthy cases of miracle fishing involved the 1994 kidnapping of US agricultural expert Thomas Hargrove at a roadblock outside Cali, Colombia. Hargrove subsequently spent 11 months in captivity. The movie Proof of Life was largely based on the Hargrove case. The movie dramatically depicts a miracle fishing/mass kidnapping incident.

In some cases victims are abducted in mass from a fixed location. I know of one case anecdotally in the early 2000s where the patrons of a roadside restaurant, also outside Cali were kidnapped en masse. They were given rubber boots and marched into the jungle. There each person was assessed and the valuable fish were retained and the others released.

Its important to understand the potential risk of miracle fishing kidnaps because a lot of the things we may do for crime prevention and kidnap avoidance like watching for surveillance, varying routes, etc. will not necessarily help. Situational awareness will still be important though. If you come upon a roadblock suddenly you will have very limited time to determine your best course of action and probably very limited options.

Hotel and Restaurant Takeovers

Following up on the miracle fishing kidnapping discussion its a good opportunity to discuss other situations where victims are seized in masse as many of the same issues exist. These are also crimes that, like miracle fishing are circumstances where fundamental security measures may be of limited use.

For this reason we'll look at different examples of this from hotel takeovers in Lagos, Nigeria to recent restaurant takeovers in Sao Paulo, Brazil.

Recently there have been a rash of restaurant takeovers and armed robberies in Sao Paulo, Brazil. The phenomenon is called arrastao - Portuguese for "trawling" - and while it has been going on for several years but has recently increased in frequency. The arrastao gangs - usually composed of four to ten men - select a target based on the ease of entry and exits and then descend at a peak hour when the establishment is full of diners. They move in quickly, secure the restaurant and rob the patrons and employees at gunpoint taking anything of value that they can get - usually cash, jewelry and electronic items. The robbery is usually over within minutes and the gang withdraws as quickly as they have arrived.

Lagos, Nigeria has experienced a similar - and perhaps more violent - pattern of hotel takeovers. These incidents while more common around 2007-2009 are still occurring - at least as recently as 2011 when the Imperial Hotel in Lagos was invaded and guests, including a prominent Nigerian actress were robbed at gunpoint. While many of the hotels that were robbed were guesthouses and small budget hotels, one popular brand hotel was also taken over on Ikoyi island in Lagos. In some of these Nigerian cases the robbery gangs have actually gone door-to-door in the hotels robbing guests in their rooms.

Incidents like the Mumbai attacks - where the intent was to kill as many people as possible and the temporary assault on an upscale Rio de Janeiro hotel by rival gangs are a little bit different but some of the fundamental precautions are the same. In hotel takeover situations once you become of aware of the situation you have basically two options: (1) get out quickly without being noticed or (2) shelter-in-place. If you are in a restaurant that is taken over you will likely have limited to no option to shelter in place (unless you are in or near the restroom) and very likely no opportunity to escape as the attack will be planned out well and the perpetrators will likely have secured all the exits. Fortunately these are usually economically motivated crimes and if you surrender your valuables the criminals will likely take what they can get and want to leave as quickly as possible.

Shelter in place for a situation like a hotel takeover will be the same as for an active shooter situation. You will want to seek both cover (protection from gunfire, etc.) and concealment (protection from observation).

The bottom line is that like miracle fishing these types of events are difficult to counter using many of the fundamental individual protective measures. The best defense is to know the local patterns and trends, the profiles of establishments that are being attacked and avoid being there. Awareness will still be a key component and if all else fails may help you at least recognize the danger more rapidly.

Nothing Good Happens After Midnight

This may be a generality but all-in-all its a good rule of thumb. In some countries it might be better to say 1am and in others maybe 10pm but the principle is sound.

Especially when traveling abroad its important to be cautious about your alcohol intake as this affects your judgment, your ability to respond and generally makes you more likely to be a victim of crime or even social violence. As you -- and others around you become more intoxicated the potential for trouble increases. Social violence -- often manifesting itself through barroom confrontations with other patrons and similar activities -- can be potentially very dangerous. Writer and corrections officer Rory Miller describes these types of social confrontations as the "monkey dance" drawing parallels between human behavior and that of our simian cousins. You don't want to do the monkey dance - or worse the "group monkey dance" in a bar in your home town let alone a bar thousands of miles away where cultural and language barriers can fuel the confrontation and potentially the violence. The best way to avoid these types of situations is to avoid these types of establishments, especially after a certain time of the evening when a significant percentage of the patrons may be drunk.

A frequent scam in many cities around the world is for people on the street, sometimes handing out flyers to lure you in to a bar or nightclub where you are then presented with a huge bill for overpriced drinks. When you try to protest you will likely be confronted by several large gentlemen who will not permit you to leave until you settle the bill. The best way to avoid this is to not allow yourself to be lured into bars or nightclubs by overly aggressive touts and to check drink prices before ordering. Local police will usually be unhelpful and unlikely to intervene in these situations.

Another old adage that usually holds true is that if you look for trouble you will probably find it. If you are wandering around a strange city at night looking for companionship, drugs or whatever else you are likely to find yourself on a bad situation.

If you do go out late at night go out in a group and choose your companions wisely. Have a transportation plan to get you back to your hotel or other accommodation safely and limit the amount of valuables you are carrying so that if you are robbed the result will not be catastrophic.

Active Shooter Situations

One of the most dangerous situations you can encounter at home or abroad is an active shooter scenario. Particularly since the Columbine School shooting US law enforcement has devoted a great deal of effort on training to deal with active shooter situations. This phenomenon has occurred over and over again - most notably as of this writing with the Colorado movie theatre shooting. This is not a uniquely American experience as active shooter situations have occurred in different places around the world. In some of the foreign cases the "active shootings" are actually militant attacks on soft targets.

Two examples of particular concern for travelers are the January 2008 attack on the Serena Hotel in Kabul, Afghanistan and the 2008 attacks in Mumbai, India. In both cases the attackers breached hotels (the Mumbai attacks also involved other soft targets) and victimized guests.

While these attacks had pre-incident indicators they likely would not be visible to a short-term hotel guest. Therefore - as with most of the types of situations we have discussed before - the best immediate defense is awareness. As soon as you become aware that an active shooter situation is occurring you typically have to choose quickly between two options: (1) evacuate (2) shelter in place. If conditions permit and you can do it safely it's usually best to evacuate the building under attack and move to a safe location. The difficulty with this option is that frequently too much may be unclear to make a good decision. Has the shooter or shooters blocked the exits? Have they set up fields of fire on the likely evacuation routes, hoping to draw people into a killzone? In many cases you may have to go for option 2, to shelter in place.

When sheltering in place it's important to consider cover and concealment. How do they differ? Cover is any object that will protect your body from gunfire, shrapnel and other projectiles. Concealment protects your body against visibility and detection. Both are important. Some objects will offer both cover and concealment, some will offer one but not the other. Whenever possible you want both. Also as with any defensive position you want to use a layered approach if you can. As an example, if you become aware of an active shooter threat you might seek shelter in a closed, locked office or your hotel room if you are in a hotel. This will provide you concealment (unless of course it's a glass office) and possibly a minor barrier (the locked door). Once inside the office you can seek cover and in fact additional concealment by going behind a large desk or other piece of furniture. You should silence your cell phone, watch alarm or any other electronic device that might emit noise and give away your location. You should also try to arm yourself with an improvised weapon of some type and prepare yourself mentally should you be discovered and have to attack the shooter as a last ditch effort. If possible you should call a reliable contact or an emergency number for the police and advise them of the situation. Be cautious however about revealing your location. If it's a lone shooter then it's probably useful to the responding police to know where you are located. However in a more complex terrorist event, like the Mumbai Attacks the attackers maybe using scanners to monitor first responder radio transmissions and cell phone calls. There is a risk – although maybe remote – that they may intercept your call and therefore know the location where you are hiding. Unfortunately you likely won't know the nature of the attack when it occurs. You may have to make your decision based on the location where you are, what the likely threats are and their potential capabilities.

Additional resources are the US Department of Homeland Security Active Shooter Response Guide (http://www.dhs.gov/xlibrary/assets/active_shooter_booklet.pdf) and pocket card (http://www.dhs.gov/xlibrary/assets/active_shooter_pocket_card.pdf) and the NYPD Active Shooter Recommendations and Analysis for Risk Mitigation (http://www.nyc.gov/html/nypd/downloads/pdf/counterterrorism/Act iveShooter.pdf

Civil Unrest

Civil unrest can be one of the most difficult challenges you may face in international travel and can be one of the times when you may truly be a random victim of circumstance. One of the best ways to prepare for civil unrest is to know the location where you are traveling. Some places have a history of political unrest and civil disturbance and there may be patterns and trends that you can learn from. These may relate to particular times of year or trigger events that spark unrest or specific hotspots or focal points where crowds often gather and unrest is likely to occur.

It's important to note, however that this is not always the case and past history is not necessarily indicative of future events. Perhaps the most dramatic example of this was the Arab Spring. The Arab Spring was an eye-opener and in many ways a game changer for many security professionals, governments and businesses. Notions of clearly discernible trip wires or trigger points that would provide significant indication of a deterioration in the local environment were turned upside down.

Perhaps largely due to the use of social media and the rapid flow of information to a wide audience, events during the Arab Spring moved at a pace that was so quick it left many organizations and individuals struggling to catch up. Regional governments that were largely perceived as stable folded surprisingly quickly and governments that endured still face significant challenges that came to forefront during this period.

If you are in a location where civil unrest occurs, and in particular if it is widespread and unfolds rapidly you will normally have two options: evacuate or shelter-in-place. Which option to take will depend largely on the particular situation and circumstances. Many times if you are at a safe location it is best to stay there until conditions stabilize. Trying to get to the airport or cross a border while running a gauntlet of angry mobs or warring factions will likely further jeopardize your safety. Conversely if you are not in a safe location and are not able to get to a safe location or if you have sufficient lead time then evacuation might be the better option. This is especially true if the situation is likely to get progressively worse.

Contingency Planning

Always Have An Exit Plan

When traveling or living in the politically unstable regions it's important to always have an exit plan. After assessing the potential threats from coups, civil unrest or conflict you should consider several methods of egress from the country, different transportation modes that could be used and also the possibility of sheltering in place.

You should consider some tripwires or triggerpoints that might indicate a deterioration in the security situation and be a signal to you to act on. your exit plan. These vary greatly depending on the country and the situation there but some examples might be: departure of dependents and non-essential personnel from diplomatic missions, imposition of martial law, previously peaceful demonstrations turn violent, etc.

The events of the Arab Spring taught us - tripwires can be much more compressed than anticipated. With the introduction on social media in particular political and security conditions can change very rapidly.

Under ideal circumstances your exit plan is to go to the airport before the situation becomes too bad and board a scheduled commercial flight and leave the country. You do need to consider other options should the airport be closed or unreachable. Other possibilities might be traveling overland across the border to a neighboring country or even a maritime mode of departure such as hiring a charter boat if the country isn't landlocked and if there is a safe haven country reachable by boat.

You should stay in contact with your Embassy or Consulate if they have representation locally. The US State Department issues messages to it citizens who have registered with the Embassy and prepares to conduct evacuations should the situation warrant it. This can also be a good indicator or tripwire to use. The US State Department, British Foreign and Commonwealth Office and other countries foreign ministries try to encourage their citizens to depart the country as soon as they feel the situation is becoming critical in order to ease the burden should an evacuation be necessary.

In some cases immediate exit may not be possible or safe. Borders maybe closed as occurred during and after the coup in Mali in 2012 or the situation may have destabilized so rapidly that it is not safe to be out on the streets or moving around. In those situations its important to look at sheltering in place.
When preparing to shelter in place you should stockpile enough food and water in your hotel room, house or apartment to sustain you for several days. Its difficult to determine what length of time to anticipate but 72-96 hours is a good general rule. You will also want to have a flashlight, batteries, possibly a battery powered radio, cell phone and or Sat/com phone and associated chargers. A portable battery-powered cell phone charger is also a good option as well.

The level of planning and preparation will vary greatly depending upon the conditions in the country you are in and your personal situation. Even giving this topic some thought and some minimal planning will give you a head start should things turn bad and you will be better off that if you were caught totally unprepared.

Dealing with Local Police

Dealing with Police in the Developing World

Most of us raised in the US and other democracies have been taught from an early age to seek out a police officer for assistance when they have a problem. Unfortunately this is not always the best course of action in the developing world. In these locations police and other security forces are often best avoided. Frequently the best case scenario is that the police will be incompetent -- under-trained and poorly funded. In some locations there are cases where the police are unable to respond to incidents because they have no fuel for their vehicles. It's also typical to expect some level of corruption on the part of the police who are usually underpaid and in some instances may literally need to partake in at least petty corruption to earn a living wage. In the worst cases, the police are sometimes also involved in criminal activity - Mexico and the Philippines are two countries offhand where there have been issues with this. In both of those countries off-duty and even active duty police have been involved with kidnap for ransom gangs and of course the extensive ties between serving members of Mexican law enforcement and the drug trafficking organizations has been widely reported and is well known.

In some places in the Islamic world there are ties between members of the police/security forces and militant jihadists. The paradox in countries like Yemen and Pakistan is that one element of the security forces is fiercely fighting the militants while another element is sympathizing or colluding with them.

These factors should be taken into account when encountering law enforcement and security forces overseas. Expectations that police response will be like what you are accustomed to at home will likely leave you disappointed. Remember to that interaction with police in some countries can increase your risk not lower it.

Not in Kansas Anymore…..

One of the greatest challenges in protecting a global workforce and training travelers and personnel undertaking overseas assignments is getting them to understand that the individual rights they enjoy in their home country don't travel with them overseas. This is particularly true of Americans who are imbued from an early age with the concept of individual freedoms and civil rights. These are noble qualities that are unfortunately absent in much of the world.

When Americans and other citizens of western democracies travel abroad for the most part their individual rights do not travel with them. In a foreign country you are subject to local laws whether you agree with them or not and if you break them there is very little your embassy can do to assist you. Concepts like innocent until proven guilty, beyond a reasonable doubt, fair and speedy trial and so forth are alien in many foreign countries. The embassy or consulate may be able to assist with finding you legal representation and will visit you to check on your health and well being but will likely be powerless to assist you beyond that. You could languish for weeks or months in confinement before even seeing a judge. This is more of a concern in developing nations and less so in other democracies - although Amanda Knox who was tried for murder in Italy would probably disagree with that statement. Regardless of your opinion of Knox's innocence or guilt and although she was ultimately released few would say she got a fair trial or fair treatment in the Italian legal system.

We touched on this briefly before in our discussion about personal security myths but it is well worth addressing in greater detail. It is such a common and pervasive vulnerability - especially with novice travelers that it warrants closer examination.

It's important to know about the local laws and social mores of the place where you are visiting, working or living. This means understanding that some behavior and activities that are perfectly legal and acceptable at home may be illegal in the country where you are located. Even if you are not technically breaking a law you may be violating a social taboo or custom that can cause problems for you. Many people use language "respect for the local culture". I don't like this particular verbiage as it implies a level of agreement or acceptance of the particular culture. That culture may include denying women the right to an education and other basic rights, use of child soldiers, capital punishment for adultery and other things that are reprehensible. I don't think these things need to be "respected" but we do need to be aware of their place in the local landscape and our inability to change them.

For your own safety and self preservation though you do need to be aware of potential pitfalls. I also don't want to overstate the problem and give the impression that foreign jails are full of innocent Americans and other westerners. Let's be clear: a large number of the western citizens imprisoned overseas are in jail for drug offenses and the majority are guilty. They may be serving sentences or under conditions that seem harsh by our standards but most are guilty. That said there are people detained for crimes that would not be considered illegal in most western democracies.

Here are some areas that can cause you to inadvertently break local laws and run afoul of local authorities. I have intentionally omitted blatant crimes that are illegal almost everywhere like drug trafficking. Obviously there is a lot of variation from country to country:

Involvement in local politics. Becoming involved in local politics by supporting one political party or another, advocating democracy and things of that nature are likely to draw unwanted attention from local police and security forces as well as militias and other informal groups supporting the ruling or opposition party. I recognize that some non-governmental organizations (NGOs) have this specific type of activity as their mission. In those cases its strongly recommended that the organization complete a risk assessment and have a security and contingency plan.

Proselytizing: Spreading religious messages, holding religious services and attempting to convert local people is considered criminal in many countries - in particular, but not exclusively in the Muslim world. Again - I recognize this is the specific mission of many faith-based groups. As with NGOs mentioned above its strongly recommended that the organization complete a risk assessment and have a security and contingency plan.

Questionable business ventures and partners. We will go into greater detail on this topic in another section. Suffice to say getting involved with questionable business dealings and partners can create local legal troubles for you. Also unscrupulous local partners, customers or vendors can use the local legal system to their advantage to gain leverage in business disputes.

Photographing critical infrastructure and government buildings. Behavior that could be mistaken for intelligence gathering may cause you to be arrested and charged with espionage. Taking pictures or airports, military bases, presidential residences, government buildings and the like can get you into a great deal of trouble. This is especially true in the coup-prone countries of Sub-Saharan Africa. In fairness to those governments that type of activity can be mistaken for reconnaissance. Foreigners arrested, imprisoned and horribly tortured in Equatorial Guinea in 2004 were in fact an advance team planning to overthrow the ruler of that country.

Adoption. Adoption in some foreign countries can be a perilous process if not done correctly and in coordination with reputable organizations. Some governments have viewed adoption efforts as human trafficking. In one recent case in West Africa an American couple was detained on suspicion of human trafficking and were only released after high level diplomatic involvement.

Public Drunkenness. In a number of countries in the Middle East -- even some where alcohol is permitted public drunkenness is a serious crime.

Religious/Social Infractions: These include things such as

inappropriate dress, public displays of affection, adultery, possession of literature or media deemed "pornography" by local standards. Several Gulf countries impose fines and even confinement for Ramadan offenses (even by foreigners/non-Muslims).

Its important to keep in mind that when in a foreign country you are subject to its laws and behave accordingly.

Medical Considerations of Travel Abroad

While our focus has largely been on pure security issues and medical situations are arguably more safety than security focused its still worthy of some mention and its a critical component of personal safety.

It's safe to say that most travelers and expatriates are far more likely to fall victim to an accident or illness when overseas rather than a violent criminal incident or terrorist attack. For this reason it's important to be forewarned with knowledge about potential medical hazards at your destination and have some contingency plans.

With a few exceptions its safe to say that most medical care in the developing world does not come close to what most of us are accustomed to in the West. There are some notable exceptions and some places that are known for "medical tourism" where travelers specifically go to receive medical procedures that are more affordable and still considered to be good quality. There are also places where there are western-trained and educated physicians and medical staff although good equipment and facilities may be lacking.

Many places however are lacking in both trained staff and good facilities - particularly in Sub-Saharan Africa and Central Asia. In many of these locations an injury or an infection that could be easily treated at home could be fatal. There may not be an effective emergency medical service and ambulance response may be slow or non-existent. Poor sanitary conditions may also make the local hospital a dangerous place where your condition may get worse, not better.

For these reasons it's important to have a viable contingency plan for dealing with medical emergencies -- from basic prevention potentially up to medical evacuation.

Basic Prevention:

Inoculations: find out what diseases are common at your destination and what inoculations are available for them. Also find out what shots are required and carry a shot card as proof you have received them. Yellow Fever vaccination as an example is required by a number of countries. If you are not vaccinated or cannot prove you are vaccinated by producing a valid shot card some African countries will administer the vaccine to you in the airport under questionable sanitary conditions.

Malaria Prophylaxis: If traveling to a malaria-prone area you should consider whether or not to take an anti-malarial drug such as Malarone or something similar. Regardless you should bring and use insect repellent as well as limiting your outdoor activity and night, wearing long-sleeved shirts, pants, etc. These measures will also protect you against other mosquito-borne diseases like Dengue Fever.

Pack a first aid kit: Bring a small first aid kit with Bandaids, antiseptic, lomatide/Immodium (given the high likelihood of gastrointestinal disorders). Ensure none of the components of your first aid kit are considered prohibited items or controlled drugs at your destination.

Don't drink the water: Or brush your teeth with it. Use bottled water from a trusted source.

Avoid green vegetables, peeled fruit, etc.: Avoid salads and other greens unless you are sure of the sanitary conditions during preparation. Avoid fruits and vegetables unless you peel them yourself or wash them yourself with bottled water.

Eat moderate portions: Don't arrive in a new country and gorge yourself on the local chow.

Use hand sanitizer: Self explanatory. Keep yourself and your hands in particular as clean as possible.

Wear your seatbelt: That sounds like a no-brainer but the implications of a motor vehicle accident overseas can be much more significant than at home.

Medical Care:

Medical Facilities: Try to determine the level, capability and quality of local medical facilities prior to arrival or when you first get there. In many places the best choice is a private clinic. Determine what criteria there is to get treated at the clinic in advance of a problem occurring. In some places there are no acceptable facilities and you will need to be evacuated. Find all this out before a problem occurs.

Payment: Many overseas medical facilities will require payment, sometimes in cash, before treatment is rendered. Again -- develop a plan for this before the situation arises.

Evacuation: Determine how you will get evacuated and to where if your medical condition warrants it.

There are a number of providers that provide emergency medical assistance abroad such as Global Rescue, International SOS, Frontier Medex, TravelMed and others. This is not an endorsement of any of them but they may be worth looking into to address some of these issues.

Dealing with Local Contacts

Security Considerations When Working with Local Contacts

If you are working overseas or traveling internationally for business then you probably deal with local contacts of some type. They may be local representatives, partners, vendors or suppliers, customers or others. While most interaction with local contacts will be valuable and productive there are potential security concerns to be aware of and to think about.

For this discussion we won't be looking closely at fraud or compliance issues associated with the Foreign Corrupt Practices Act (FCPA), UK Bribery Act or similar legislation. Those are very worthy issues to examine but well beyond the scope of this discussion. Instead we'll look at some of the other concerns that can arise.

It goes without saying that you should do a thorough due diligence on local contacts but the reality is that you may not be able to achieve it in every situation based on the timeline or other factors. Also -- to be frank -- the ability to do an effective due diligence in many locations is very limited - especially on short notice.

Its reasonable to expect that at a minimum your contact will have a different perspective and world view than you do. There will likely be different expectations or what is acceptable. In some cases though the contact may have a separate agenda or hidden motives that can put you at risk.

Some situations that can occur that you should be aware of:

Misrepresentation: Local contacts that misrepresent themselves or their affiliation with your organization. If they engage in illegal activity while misrepresenting themselves it can have direct and severe implications for your and your company.

Allegations of criminal or unethical conduct against you or your organization: customers, vendors or others can put pressure on you by alleging misconduct to local law enforcement authorities.

Honey traps: Local contacts may try to put you in compromising positions with local women -- either to create a situation where they can blackmail you outright or at least make you vulnerable to them.

Unlawful detention: In some cases local contacts may detain you -- either physically or through use of threats -- to get you to agree to their terms.

Kidnapping: In extreme circumstances your contacts may set you up for kidnap for ransom. There was a notable case in Mexico about 10 years ago where a US businessman was set-up for a kidnapping by his Mexican partner.

Guilt by association: In some instances your contacts may be involved in activities that make them a target of law enforcement, criminal groups or both. If you are with them you may be the victim of arrest or a violent attack.

Hidden ties: In some cases your local contacts may have ties to foreign intelligence services or extremist groups. Even though they may not act against you immediately they may be gathering information about you or your organization.

How can you mitigate your exposure to these potential threats?

Of course the first answer is know who you are dealing with -- but as we discussed earlier that is not always too easy.

One thing you can do is not put all your eggs in one basket. It's not uncommon for local contacts to make some or all of your arrangements when you are visiting their country -- often everything from your hotel to your ground transportation. I suggest you may not want to always let them do it. It takes more work but if you make your own arrangements it gives you greater flexibility. If you have your own ground transportation set up apart from them it is easier to come and go as you please. You should also consider making other appointments and establishing other contacts while there. This gives you a legitimate reason to excuse yourself if a situation becomes uncomfortable and it reduces the control they have over you. Many of the scenarios outlined above are more likely to occur if you are completely dependent on them. If you have other contacts and your own transportation it goes a long way to keeping them off-balance. They don't know who you know or who you may be able to turn to for assistance. It may sound excessive or paranoid but compartmentalizing your activities gives you more control and if your contacts have bad intentions it can make it more difficult for them to act against you.

You should also make sure that someone in your head office, your family or both has all the names and contact information for the people you are planning to meet with and any itinerary you may have. In a worst case scenario if you go missing there will at least be some baseline information to use in initiating a search.

Summary & Key Points

The goal of this book has been to enhance your personal security and your understanding of measures that you can take especially when traveling or living abroad that can significantly reduce your risk.

In conclusion it's helpful to review the key points that were discussed throughout the different chapters. Understanding and applying the critical elements of personal security will go a long way to making you safer.

Situational Awareness: One aspect that has come up repeatedly throughout the book has been the concept of situational awareness. More than any other thing you can do, being aware of your surroundings and being able to identify potential threats will help keep you safe. Knowing when to increase your level of alertness will allow you to be more focused at potentially vulnerable times and locations and will help you avoid the fatigue of being hyper-alert all the time.

Know the Local Threat Environment: By knowing the local situation in terms of crime and other threats you will be better prepared to mitigate or counter these threats. This includes understanding crime trends, modus operandi and dangerous areas.

Perform a Personal Risk Assessment: Based on your knowledge of the local threat environment look at your daily activities and routine and determine what the risk is to you. Once these risks are identified consider ways to reduce or mitigate them.

Understand Fundamental Individual Protective Measures:
Understand the basics of route analysis and route selection, detecting surveillance and potential threats, protecting operational and personal security information, etc. and apply these principles in your

daily life. Even doing this at a very rudimentary level will go a long way towards reducing risk.

Contingency Plan: Planning for a variety of possible scenarios and situations will leave you much better prepared should a problem arise. Even if the situation does not exactly match the scenario you prepared for prior planning will give you a framework to adjust from.

Proper Mindsct: Realistically assessing and recognizing the threat and contingency planning will give you the confidence to properly respond to a situation and more importantly the proactive mindset to identify potential problems before they occur.

Printed in Great Britain
by Amazon